Unity

Live the day and live the moment
Pull your Karma from the torrent
Love me now — before tomorrow
Live the joy before the sorrow

Our lives rush us right past the beauty
Lift your eyes from rat race duty
See the love in our Creation
See your deeper obligation

Share your soul, get in the game
Inside ourselves, we're much the same
Drop your guard, embrace each other
We truly are sister and brother

Know the beauty of the sunrise
Find your peace — before the time flies
Life comes and goes, with or without you
Reap the joy in the time fate gives you

Live the day and live the moment
Pull your Karma from the torrent
Love me now and let me borrow,
Your gift of love — to live tomorrow
Your gift of love — to love tomorrow

Fred Sisson

EVA CASSIDY

Songbird

ROB BURLEY & JONATHAN MAITLAND

For the first time, Eva's story is told by her parents,

Hugh and Barbara Cassidy, her family and her friends.

ORION

Copyright © Rob Burley and Jonathan Maitland
and Hugh Cassidy & Barbara Cassidy 2001

The right of Rob Burley & Jonathan Maitland
to be identified as the authors of this work has been asserted
by them in accordance with the Copyright,
Designs and Patents Act 1988.

First published in Great Britain in 2001 by
ORION
An imprint of Orion Books Ltd
Orion House, 5 Upper St Martin's Lane, London WC2H 9EA

A CIP catalogue record for this book
is available from the British Library

ISBN 0 75284 779 1

Printed in Great Britain by Butler and Tanner

Photography, Art & Memorabilia Credits

Cassidy Family collection: 11-20, 22, 25, 31, 35, 37, 40, 46, 56,
59 (art), 60, 61, 62, 64, 65, 86, 89, 90, 91, 94-5 (art), 98, 119, 125,
126-7 (art), 133, 142-3, 147, 150, 157, 160
Larry Melton: 32, 39, 59, 76, 77, 85, 106, 140, 145
Anna Karen Kristinsdottir: 8, 103-5, 106 (memorabilia),
107, 112, 115-117, 135
Jackie Fletcher: 71, 73, 78, 79, 99, 110-111, 123, 130
Ned Judy: 43, 45, 49, 50, 53, 54, 57, 92
Chris Biondo: 63, 74, 75, 80, 81, 87
Maggie Haven: 121, 131
Monica Merella Steiner: 48, 67
Mark Merella: 41, 47
Ruth Murphy: 55
Elaine Stonebraker: Cover and page 93

Other Credits

Book Design: Harry Green
Literary Agent: Robert Kirby of PFD
Photographic Production: Larry Melton
Executive Editor: Elana R Byrd

Recordings

EVA CASSIDY: LIVE AT BLUES ALLEY

EVA BY HEART

SONGBIRD

TIME AFTER TIME

THE OTHER SIDE (with Chuck Brown)

Eva Cassidy Recordings are distributed by

Blix Street Records – USA

Hot Records – UK

Digeridoo Records – Aust/NZ

Dara Records – Eire

Contents

Contributors

We became involved with Eva Cassidy's story in March 2001 when we were assigned to make a short film for ITV's *Tonight With Trevor McDonald*. It was then that we realised that there was a bigger, more profound tale to tell. We would never have been able to do that without the permission of Eva's parents, Hugh and Barbara, who gave this project their blessing and wholehearted cooperation. For that we thank them and the many other members of Eva's family and close circle of friends, whose names are given here and whose words have brought her story to life. Because the people we have spoken to knew Eva so much better than anyone else, we have chosen, wherever possible, to tell her story using their words rather than ours. We hope we have done justice to the story of a remarkable talent. Rob Burley would also like to thank Moira Dustin for her hard work and Holly Dustin for her support.

ROB BURLEY AND JONATHAN MAITLAND, JULY 2001

THE FAMILY

Barbara Cassidy Eva's mother and best friend.

Hugh Cassidy Eva's father and childhood music teacher.

Anette Cassidy Eva's eldest sister. Five years older than Eva, Anette left home when Eva was eleven. They were reunited as young adults and Anette, a nurse by training, cared for Eva during her illness.

Margret Cassidy Robinson Eva's sister, born in 1962 and one year older than Eva. They attended school together through high school and had a close relationship.

Daniel Cassidy Eva's brother and eighteen months her junior. Dan shared Eva's musical interest and performed with her. He is today a professional violinist who resides in Iceland and performs frequently in the UK and Ireland.

Walter Wunderlich Eva's maternal cousin with whom she shared wonderful vacation experiences in Nova Scotia.

FRIENDS AND MUSICAL COMPANIONS

Ruth Murphy Eva's best friend at junior high school. She remained close to Eva throughout her life. Her daughter Cassidy is named after Eva.

Celia Murphy A year older than Eva, Celia met her at junior high in a folk group and remained a friend throughout her life. Celia is Ruth Murphy's elder sister.

Ned Judy The driving force behind Eva's high school group, Stonehenge, and an early boyfriend of Eva's. The two remained close and often went on trips together throughout Eva's life. Ned was one of the earliest to record Eva. He remains to this day active in music as a jazz pianist.

Larry Melton Member of Stonehenge, the high school band in which Eva sang. Lifelong friend who is today a professional musician (bass) and a professional photographer to whom we credit many photos in this book.

Mark Merella Drummer with Eva's high school group, Stonehenge. The band rehearsed in his family garage and he and Eva were briefly a couple in high school. Mark is today a professional drummer.

Monica Merella Steiner Mark's younger sister who deeply admired Eva and was nine years younger than Eva.

Elaine Stonebraker Friend with whom Eva shared art as well as biking and hiking trips in the 1990s. Fellow employee at Behnke's Nursery, Elaine took the photo which is the cover of this book and the *Songbird* CD.

Chris Biondo Eva's boyfriend and producer of much of her recorded music. He was also bass player on many of Eva's recordings.

Jackie Fletcher Friend and former housemate of Eva. She became one of Eva's most dedicated promoters and champions.

Chuck Brown The 'Godfather of Go-Go'. Brown invented Washington DC's go-go sound in the 1970s and has been leading the movement ever since. He collaborated with Eva on their 1992 album, *The Other Side*.

Anna Karen Kristinsdottir Friend at a special time in Eva's life. A young woman with whom Eva could share her aspirations and feelings. Anna Karen lives in Iceland, where Eva spent two vacations.

Lenny Williams Pianist who performed on many of Eva's recordings.

Keith Grimes Guitarist who accompanied Eva on many of her recordings.

Raice McLeod Drummer who performed on many of Eva's recordings.

Bruce Lundvall President of jazz and blues label, Blue Note.

Mick Fleetwood Drummer with rock superstars Fleetwood Mac and owner of Fleetwood's, a jazz and blues club, where Eva sang on occasion.

Grace Griffith Washington DC-based singer specialising in Celtic music. She brought Eva's music to the attention of Blix Street Records. Grace was Eva's friend late in her life.

Margaret (Maggie) Haven Eva's friend and employer from 1994 through summer of 1996. Maggie employed Eva as a mural artist and encouraged her musical career.

Kathy Oddenino Nurse and spiritual counsellor who helped Eva through the illness at the end of her life.

THE US-ENGLISH CONNECTION

Bill Straw Founder of the US Blix Street records. Signed Eva to his label posthumously. Conceived and compiled the *Songbird* and *Time After Time* albums.

Martin Jennings Managing Director of Hot Records and longtime friend of Bill Straw. Hot Records distributes Eva's CDs in the UK and Australian markets, in partnership with Blix Street Records.

Tony Bramwell Veteran record plugger who brought *Over the Rainbow* to the attention of BBC Radio 2.

Paul Walters Producer of BBC Radio 2's *Wake up to Wogan* programme and the first to play Eva's music on UK radio.

Terry Wogan BBC Radio and television presenter. Wogan played Eva's music for the first time on his *Wake up to Wogan* breakfast show.

Mark Hagen Producer, *Top of the Pops 2*. Mark Hagen took the risk of playing the amateur video of Eva performing *Over the Rainbow* on his show in November 2000 and received an unprecedented response.

Sting Superstar singer and writer of *Fields of Gold*, which Eva sings on *Live at Blues Alley* and *Songbird*.

POEMS

Fred Sisson Author of UNITY. Family friend and brother of Grace Griffith.

Elana Rhodes Byrd Author of *Song of Life*. Family friend, and Cassidy family attorney.

The Cassidy Family would like also to recognise the work of Eva's paternal cousin, *Laura Bligh*, who created and still maintains the Eva Cassidy website at http://users.erols. com/hoganandbligh/eva.htm. This site includes a Guestbook which has been an enormous source of strength and solace to the Cassidy family.

This book is warmly dedicated

to the good people of

the British Isles,

who first recognised a gem in their midst

and responded lovingly.

Barbara and Hugh Cassidy

'I was already expecting Eva at the time

and she always thought it was neat to say

she was "Made in Germany".'

Barbara Cassidy

God Bless the Child

From their backyard the Cassidy children could see the Washington Monument, centrepiece of the US capital, seven miles from their home in suburban Maryland. Eva Cassidy lived nearly all her life in the small towns and communities that radiate out from Washington DC, primarily in and around the historic town of Bowie. Her musical talent was nurtured by the area's thriving and diverse music scene, found in venues ranging from the small inns and clubs close to her home, to establishments like Blues Alley in Washington's Georgetown.

However, Eva's roots are European: her father, Hugh, is of Irish descent and her mother, Barbara, was born into a childhood of hardship in Hitler's Germany in 1939, six weeks before the outbreak of war. It was in Barbara's home town of Bad Kreuznach in the Rhineland that Eva's parents met…

Hugh Cassidy I joined the army in 1959 and for three years was a medic in a US military hospital in Germany. I met Barbara over there. She was working at the hospital on the reception desk. I liked her demeanour. She had a gentle way about her: a good, gentle soul. Six weeks after meeting, we got engaged, and then three months later, we were married – that was in March 1961.

Barbara Cassidy Hugh was stationed in my home town, Bad Kreuznach. He was a lot like my father in many ways. Intelligent, bright, and with the same values: to be your own person, to believe in what's right. When his tour of duty was over in 1962 I emigrated to the States.

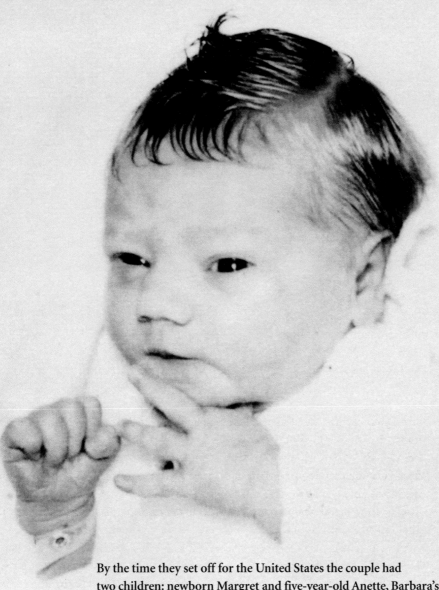

By the time they set off for the United States the couple had
two children: newborn Margret and five-year-old Anette, Barbara's child
from a previous relationship, whom Hugh would later adopt…

Eva aged two days.

Barbara Cassidy I was madly in love with my husband and never gave any thought to
leaving my family behind, going to a new country, a totally different culture. It was a very
long trip in those days with the propeller airplanes. When we landed Hugh's sister was
there, and she took this baby that I'd been holding for hours on end. And I felt I could
breathe again. I was already expecting Eva at the time and she always thought it was neat
to say she was 'Made in Germany'.

Eva Marie Cassidy, named after Hugh's grandmother, was born
in the Washington Hospital Center on 2nd February 1963.
She was taken to the family's home in the south-east of the City…

'It was really tough. We lived in a third-floor walk-up apartment with three kids. The washtubs were in the basement and Barbara had to haul all those clothes up and down. It was rough, but we were young so we could do it.'

Hugh Cassidy

Barbara Cassidy She was a very healthy baby. She had black hair when she was born. The first three months she cried quite a bit, but she was a very happy baby and smiled easily. I bought this beautiful baby carriage and put Margret at one end and Eva at the other. Margret had beautiful dark-brown eyes and copper-coloured hair and Eva was blonde with blue eyes. People would just stop me all the time and comment, 'What beautiful children.' That would make me proud.

Hugh Cassidy Barbara brought our life savings – $1600 – stuffed in her blouse on the flight over. We lived on that for two years. I played guitar, bass and gave ukelele lessons and did odd jobs, because I had to finish college during the day and play music at night. It was really tough. We lived in a third-floor walk-up apartment with three kids. The washtubs were in the basement and Barbara had to haul all those clothes up and down. It was rough, but we were young so we could do it.

But the young family were about to come close to tragedy…

Hugh Cassidy We almost lost Eva early on. She got stuck in her crib. She fell down between the railing and the bed. Eva was maybe nine, ten months. Barbara heard her cry in the morning. She walked in there and her child was hanging by the neck and blueish in the face, hanging from the crib, feet not touching the floor. She had worked her way down between the mattress and the edge of the crib.
I had just awakened and I heard Barbara say, 'My baby, my baby,' and she brought in Eva like a rag doll, all floppy and she was in tears crying, 'My baby, my baby.' Immediately she started to give mouth-to-mouth. Eva was blue, I thought that she had been like that all night. Then all of a sudden she gave a little gasp and I put her on her back on the bed and we got her going again.

LEFT
Eva at six months.

RIGHT
Hugh and Barbara
with Eva and her
sister Margret, 1963.

Anette Cassidy I was 6 years old getting ready to go to school one day and I wasn't really aware of what was going on, but Eva had somehow gotten her neck caught and she'd actually stopped breathing. Mom saw that she wasn't breathing, that she had turned blue and just tried to breathe life back into her and it worked. I remember the ambulance coming, taking her to the hospital.

Hugh Cassidy She had a convulsion or two, but two or three days later we got her back from the hospital and she was fine again. We very nearly lost her. That would have been devastating. I thought she was gone.

The couple wanted to find a home more suitable for a family with four young children, settling for a house close to the Washington city limits in suburban Maryland…

Barbara Cassidy We moved to Oxon Hill, Maryland in 1964. We bought an old frame house with half an acre of land and that's where the children got their start. It was a very quiet residential area. Hugh was teaching special education, I was busy at home raising my children. Dan was born a year and a half after Eva and those were some of the best years of my life. I really enjoyed my children.

ABOVE Eva at 2 years.

RIGHT
Margret (5) and Eva (4).

'The girls sort of hung out together and, being the boy, I would be left out sometimes. But Eva was pretty close to me. My earliest memory of Eva was her dragging me through the yard. I was a toddler and she would lead me by the hand, drag me through the yard and stop every so often to punch me lightly on the shoulder and say, "Hey Buster!"'

Dan Cassidy

Dan Cassidy The girls sort of hung out together and, being the boy, I would be left out sometimes. But Eva was pretty close to me. My earliest memory of Eva was her dragging me through the yard. I was a toddler and she would lead me by the hand, drag me through the yard and stop every so often to punch me lightly on the shoulder and say, 'Hey Buster!' That was her catchphrase at the time. I could tell that she really liked me, she paid attention to me.

Barbara Cassidy We gave them the same basic values that I had growing up: to be your own person, to be sincere and also to say 'No' when you feel it's right, even when it's not popular. We had dinner together except for two nights a week when Hugh was out in the garage lifting weights, which was very important to him. The children had to take turns doing the dishes. At first Danny said, 'I'm not going to do dishes because I am a boy,' so his sisters got on his case and made sure he got his turn too.

Hugh Cassidy Eva was the most fun-loving and happy of all the kids. You're never supposed to say this, but she was my favourite kid, simply because we had the most in common. I would get down on all fours in the horsy position and she would walk along my back out on my head and just stand there and I would see how long I could hold it.

Eva hated her itchy red wool bathing suit.

She was double-jointed. She could take her fingers and bend them all the way back. She could dislocate her shoulders at will and she could link her hands and take them all the way over, behind her back and back the other way around. She could also walk around the house on her toe knuckles, turn her toes under and just walk that way, which elevated her like a ballet dancer. I always thought it was so neat so I guess that's why she kept on doing that. She was a tomboy, she liked to get on the monkey bars and the swings and hang from her feet.

I was teaching special education and I even brought Eva to class one time when she was three or four. I don't know how I worked it into the lesson, but I had her take off her shoes and walk on her toe knuckles across my desk and do her stuff with her arms and, of course, she was just a doll-baby, real cute and the school kids all loved to see that.

Hugh's weightlifting was more than just a hobby.
In Eva's early years he was consumed by it…

Hugh Cassidy I was very disciplined with the weightlifting. I thought about it, dreamed about it, lived it, got in contests and sometimes had seven, eight quarts of milk a day and was just rabid with it. I was doing that pretty much, back in those days when they were growing up. In 1971 I was World Champion Super Heavyweight in power lifting.

Dan Cassidy He didn't spend that much time with us at that time. He was a very famous weightlifter and his goal was to be the World Champion in power lifting. When he did indeed become the World Champion, we were proud of that fact, that was for sure. His obsession was lifting weights; music was a hobby, parenting was something he did every now and again. Really my mother raised us.

Hugh with (from left)
Dan, Eva and Margret.
Ocean City, Maryland.

**Among his other parental responsibilities,
Hugh was expected to keep order in the house…**

Hugh Cassidy I was never heavy-handed with them, but they were afraid of me. I was a big fellow, I weighed 300 pounds. They told me later on that I was physically intimidating and they would do everything I said. I didn't strike them or anything, but my voice was often all I'd need. They didn't live in terror of me and we had good times together, but when they did something wrong they thought, 'Well Dad's not gonna like that.' I guess it was pretty scary, a big oaf like me.

Barbara Cassidy I think the kids were frightened of him, yes, he really was a presence.

Hugh's set of values were formed by his own upbringing…

Hugh Cassidy We tried to have the kids home for meals. My mother always had the children there. At dinnertime you were home and that was it. At suppertime we had to sit down and have time to break bread together and socialise and tell about our day. We'd go around the circle and my mother would ask, 'What did you learn today?' and we'd share it. I tried to get the kids to do that, but it wasn't easy. I could have enforced it – now my Ma would enforce it with a leather sandal. If we didn't mind our Ps and Qs we got a swat.

Margret We were raised right. I think we had a good moral upbringing.

**The proximity in age of the youngest three Cassidy children ensured
their closeness but created distance from their older sister Anette…**

Anette Cassidy I was born in Germany and came over here when I was five, Margret was very small at the time. I'm the oldest, I'm five-and-a-half years older than Eva and seven years older than Dan. It seemed like it was a big age gap. It seemed like the younger three hung out together while I went off and did my thing.

Dan Cassidy We loved our old neighbourhood, we were very happy kids. We had lots of friends. All the stores were local to us. My parents were the opposite of over-protective. They weren't particularly strict as far as leaving the yard. Some parents wouldn't let kids out of the yard, but our parents trusted us virtually one-hundred per cent in whatever we did.

Margret Cassidy Eva and I were very close. She was my favourite sibling and still is, always will be. I think a lot of that is because my brother, even though he was close in age, obviously was a boy. Then there was me and Eva side-by-side. There's just so many little things that we shared that were unique to us alone and I treasure that.

ABOVE LEFT A day's outing at Fort Washington. Margret and Eva.

ABOVE RIGHT Eva and Dan.

In our backyard, my Dad didn't cut the grass that often, which was to our delight as children. When we were real little we would hide in the grass and pretend we were bunny rabbits. Our backyard was really beautiful. I have good memories of our old house in Oxon Hill.

Appreciation of nature was always of great importance to both Barbara and Hugh and they believed it was essential to teach their children about the natural world…

Hugh Cassidy Nature has always been a hobby of mine, so on the weekends we always took the kids out for walks. They learned how to identify plants and trees rather early on. We had pets – turtles, fish, a pet possum one time, and ducks. We raised bees and I had hogs outside.

Barbara Cassidy When Eva was a little child there were particular little flowers that were very minute but, children being so close to the ground, she saw them and made me little bouquets, which she brought to me. We also had a vegetable garden. She saw how tomatoes first blossom, then ripen. There were also cherry trees. We took the children out on nature walks on Sunday.

Dan Cassidy My mother almost insisted that as a family every Sunday we'd all go for a walk in a nice nature area that wasn't far away. A little place called Cedarville, a park with cedar trees and a pond and walkways. That was our favourite place, apart from going to the shopping mall.

Eva had a lifelong passion and gift for art and artistic creativity and these talents were apparent from an early age…

ABOVE LEFT Front porch, 2010 Owens Road. Eva, Dan, Margret, Anette.

ABOVE RIGHT Ferry to Tangier Island, Maryland. From left: Anette, Margret, Dan, Eva aged 6 and Barbara.

Barbara Cassidy We always provided paper and crayons and pencils for the children and we could tell that even by the age of two, or two-and-a-half, her stick-people were very pronounced.

Hugh Cassidy The artistic stuff came along first, long before music. Her scribbles seemed to have a little more to them than the average kid's. Her stick-figures were amazingly lifelike – even though they were still stick-figures and obviously the work of a child. They had motion and feeling about them that we recognised. She had a natural talent for figures and movement.

Margret Cassidy I think while other kids were doing just everyday stuff like playing – which she did with us of course – she had her own little things going on, even at a young

Eva while at elementary school.

age. She would like to draw and she liked to be by herself sometimes. Just to do her own little thing.

Barbara Cassidy To introduce them to art I would take them down into Washington, where there were these beautiful museums, such as the National Gallery of Art. At the end of each visit they could get a postcard, a reproduction of whatever picture they liked best. She would draw just anything, whatever grabbed her. For a while she drew beautiful delicate fairies. It was an innate talent and she always had ideas bubbling in her head and she couldn't execute them fast enough.

Dan Cassidy We all went to the same elementary school in Oxon Hill. It was right down the street and children would walk there. She entered a school talent show and she got right up there and drew a nice picture. She did it very calmly and she did not waste one moment, she didn't stop, she just drew. When she showed it to the audience she got an excellent round of applause. I was very impressed because I was right there in the audience.

Margret Cassidy She just got up there with her sketch pad and drew a beautiful picture of a clown real quick. Everyone was just really amazed, because here's this little kid who's like a real artist. At that point I think my parents realised, 'Oh she's really going to do something with this; she's really talented.'

Eva's family also recall that she was an unusually sensitive and compassionate child…

Barbara Cassidy She was very sensitive. She saw Ray Charles on television when she was three or four and she said, 'Mommy, why is he wearing those dark glasses?' I said, 'Well, the man is blind and maybe he just feels better with those glasses on.' She was almost in tears. She said, 'But how's he going to get home, if he can't see?' She was very compassionate. If the kids did something and they got in trouble, she told me later in life that sometimes she took the blame, because she didn't want any of her siblings to get in trouble for it.

Margret Cassidy One thing you can say of her was that she was such a kind person. She never got in trouble for doing anything mean or saying anything mean. She didn't have that in her. And I really admire her for that, because I can't think of too many people who don't do or say mean things. But she didn't.

Barbara Cassidy However, she could be stubborn. She could also get angry sometimes. Her face would get red and then she would stomp her foot. We used to call this her 'Rumpelstiltskin act'. I picked out a pink dress for her when she was in the first grade. I thought it was really lovely and I insisted that she wear it.
A few weeks later I saw a cut in the hem of the dress and Eva said, 'I don't know how it got there.' Many, many years later she told me, 'I hated that dress so much that I took the scissors and cut it.'

Like millions of other kids growing up in America in the 1960s, the Cassidy kids were influenced by pop culture and fashion…

Barbara Cassidy What they watched on television was very important and they tried to play-act, especially Cher, who made such a big impression. There was a show, *The Sonny and Cher Show*, and Eva and Margret absolutely adored Cher with her long hair, but when the girls were little I had short, pixie haircuts for them.

Margret Cassidy We always wanted to have long hair. Cher was one of our idols and she had long hair. So since we didn't have long hair, we'd put towels on our heads and have them hanging down and pretend like we had long hair and that we were singing. She was really our idol because she did the music, she had long hair, she wore glamorous dresses, and she was famous. So that's someone we wanted to be.

Music was always important in the children's lives. Hugh was a keen record buyer and a professional musician who performed at the weekends…

Hugh Cassidy I started the kids on folk songs. The folk-music craze, of course, came in the 1950s and 1960s and it was ongoing while rock was going on. She was born in 1963, so it was her early childhood that was really the folkie era. We had a very good folk record collection. We got the Folkways records, Leadbelly, the Weavers, I was playing bass, guitar and ukulele at the time with the 'Collegians' doing high school proms and college dances.

Margret Cassidy We always had music going on. My parents bought a new stereo and they were so excited. We were, too. It was a big deal, getting the latest stereo equipment. So there were a certain few records that we'd hear over and over. One was *Bob Dylan's Greatest Hits* and Eva liked Buffy Sainte-Marie. Of course, the radio would also be on. My Dad had a garage that he converted into a gym for weightlifting and he'd have the radio going. While we were growing up we always had music around us.

Dan Cassidy There was music on the phonograph all the time. My mother was an
avid music listener. I'd say more so than my Dad, so that has an influence. She listened to
mainly folk music. Her favourite singers were Harry Belafonte and Pete Seeger.
Those were records she played over and over. Not to us, but for her own enjoyment.

Eva and Margret.

Barbara Cassidy We had LPs of our favourite singers – Pete Seeger, Bob Dylan – and
the children would play them. We had this coffee table and there was little Eva and
Margret and Dan and that song *Everybody Must Get Stoned*. They would play this and
march around the coffee table having absolutely no idea what this guy was saying, but
they had such a grand time!

**The range of music available to Eva as she grew up was extensive
and was not limited to recordings. Performing was always part of the culture
Eva's father created in the family home…**

Dan Cassidy Dad must have known hundreds, literally hundreds, of tunes. Old tunes, folk
music and music that was non-commercial. I think that my parents introduced Eva to that.
That had a huge effect on Eva and myself because a lot of kids only liked what was on the
radio. It's normal; they're expected to; they're lured into it almost by peer pressure. So they
don't really develop a taste for music and Eva wasn't one of those persons, that's for sure.

Anette Cassidy Dad, of course, is a musician. And I remember from a very young age
him getting all of us together and he'd be playing either the banjo or the guitar. I think
he was even into mandolins for a while. He'd get us singing folk songs mostly.

Barbara Cassidy The children always played and sang. They all had nice singing
voices and they would learn songs in school and they would bring them home and sing.
Hugh got together with them and they sang three- or four-part harmonies together,
and, at family gatherings, with the extended family. They would do little performances
and Hugh supervised that.

Dan Cassidy There was music at the dinner table. My Dad taught us four-part
harmonies. Now most kids of that age can't carry a tune and if they can, that's as far
as it goes. We had to memorise parts. Now my Dad only knew this from traditions of
barber-shop harmony singing. Our big number was a song called *Tell Me Why the Stars
do Shine*. It's an ancient tune. And we actually were able to sing a four-part harmony.
It was a new experience and it sounded good. We were proud of ourselves for memorising
our parts. By no means was it any more than just a fun little thing at the dinner table.
I do remember once a friend of my Dad's was over for dinner and Dad said, 'Why don't
we do that number that we've been working on? You ready? Hit it!' and we did it.
I suppose technically that was our first performance as the Cassidys.

Hugh Cassidy They all seemed to react pretty well to the music when we started.
I wasn't thinking about a family band at the beginning. I was just thinking, wouldn't
it be nice, since I liked to sing, if we could do some harmony singing. So I lined the kids
up so that we could do four-part harmony. Sometimes Anette would join us.

Anette Cassidy He would get Eva singing the different harmony parts. I was young
but I can remember just being so struck by how easy it was for her. And I would
try to do it but I couldn't, and I thought, 'How could she do that?' It just all came
naturally to her.

Margret Cassidy One of my memories of childhood is when, after dinner, we'd go
in the living room, and we'd sing, and my father would try to get us to do barber-shop
quartet-type stuff. We could do anything from a modern song to an old-fashioned song
to a religious hymn. The variety was really good and we enjoyed it. It was fun.
I think that's when Dad enjoyed his children the most, the music thing.

Hugh Cassidy As the time went on it was obvious that Eva had more of a gift for
singing. Later on she had the ability to harmonise with just about anything. She always
sang harmony to the tunes on the TV or the radio and we sang what was in the record
collection. On all the car trips we took she was always singing something. We got together
quite often in the early years, when they were kids, and I taught them how to modulate
to a different key. As soon as she heard me take the melody into that key, she was right
there with the harmony.

'As the time went on it was obvious that she had more of a gift for singing. Later on she had the ability to harmonise with just about anything. She always sang harmony to the tunes on the TV or the radio and we sang what was in the record collection. On all the car trips we took she was always singing something. We got together quite often in the early years, when they were kids, and I taught them how to modulate to a different key. As soon as she heard me take the melody into that key, she was right there with the harmony.'

Hugh Cassidy

**It was at this time that Eva first expressed a desire to become a singer
and identified singers she admired or aspired to be...**

Barbara Cassidy She was especially taken with Buffy Sainte-Marie, who sang
Tall Trees in Georgia. Eva always loved that song ever since and later performed it.

Dan Cassidy Buffy Sainte-Marie wore a cowboy hat and had beautiful, long hair. She was
very exotic-looking for us. When Eva was about seven, she was looking at the back of this
Buffy Sainte-Marie album, called *I'm Gonna be a Country Girl Again*, and there was a
distinctive picture of Buffy with headphones on recording in front of a microphone.
Eva told me, 'When I first looked at that picture I immediately thought to myself, Hey,
this is what I want to do.' She also had a record by Judy Collins and I think that these two
women were her earliest influences. Eva was not one to be enamoured of singers on the
radio, which was an early sign that she was not particularly into commercial music.

**In 1972, when Eva was nine, the family moved fifteen miles from Oxon Hill to Bowie,
which at that time was a semi-rural community ideal for bringing up young children ...**

Margret Cassidy Originally, before we came along in the early 1960s, Bowie was a lot
of farmland and swampland and it stayed like that probably for a good twenty years.
We were especially lucky in that our yard had more room than your typical lot. The
house we lived in was, I think, from the 1950s, before the advent of all the manufactured
homes. So our yard was a bit bigger than most in Bowie. We came from a more rustic
upbringing and atmosphere.

Dan Cassidy At around the time we moved to the new house, which was in 1972,
Eva asked if she could take up pottery, so my parents sent her to pottery class, ceramics.
She did very well at that, and that was to remain a very important part of her art-work
for the rest of her life. She worked with clay and porcelain and made little trinkets and
jewellery from that age onwards. She was always making beads and necklaces.

Eva's first day at school.

**It was at the new house in Bowie that Eva began to take an interest
in learning an instrument...**

Barbara Cassidy At first she played autoharp. Since Hugh was a musician, playing bass
professionally in a band, he had all kinds of string instruments. He'd fiddle around with
the banjo, the mandolin and the guitar. I think it was only natural that she'd show an
interest in those instruments.

Dan Cassidy The name autoharp comes from the fact that you merely press a button on
it, which presses down a chord. She picked it up right away and all of a sudden she could
sing with background and that's when my Dad taught her a repertoire of tunes. The fact
that she could accompany herself was the big breakthrough. Then it's, 'Hey, I can sing
and practise any time I want.' Then she switched to the guitar.

Hugh Cassidy I taught her guitar at nine; she picked it up very quickly. Whenever she wanted a lesson, I gave her a lesson, I showed her how to make the chords. It was a Harmony guitar, which was a low-cost, cheap brand, but it served us well for many years. It was a nylon-string guitar, easy on the fingers, so she didn't have any problem with that. I taught her *I Wish I Was a Single Girl Again*. That was one of the first tunes she learned. She could sing that as a solo when she was nine or ten. She always liked that song and later recorded it.

Dan Cassidy I had taken up the violin and it was only a matter of a short time until Eva and I made music together. So you could say we were musical partners from the very beginning. Eva and I had something in common.

Hugh Cassidy When Eva and Dan were first playing, we played as a group. By ten years old Eva knew how to play all the diminished chords on the guitar. There are only three of them and they repeat themselves, but you repeat them right on up the neck, and she thought that was real neat. The kids also knew how to do a key change in the middle of a song. I'd say, 'OK, here it comes,' and I'd look at them, and they'd look at each other and say, 'Key change,' and we'd go into the new key. Some singers don't get that until they're much older.

Eva was emerging as a talented and fun-loving child…

Dan Cassidy As a child she was almost always happy and animated and upbeat, almost to the point of being an extroverted child. She was lively, uninhibited and a talented kid. You would think nothing could ever go wrong for her as a child. She received praise gracefully; she was never afraid of anything in particular and she was always laughing and joking, even starting to do impersonations.

Barbara Cassidy She was shy around strangers, but to those people who knew her well she was quite comical and she was a lot of fun to me. She never looked for the limelight or to be number one, but she wasn't really all that shy when she felt at home with somebody. She enjoyed fairies and mermaids, that kind of fantasy – something a little unrealistic, but very beautiful and very ethereal. She liked those kind of things.

Dan Cassidy We were children of the television. We were raised by that thing. If any kids were raised with the TV, we were. It was a very important part of our life. We sat on the sofa and watched TV all day long. We were lazy kids. My Mum had to work and so did my Dad, so we got home from school early and turned on the TV right away and when my Dad got home he'd say, 'You kids sit on your butts all day and do nothing.'

Margret Cassidy We did watch a lot of TV, much more so than my Dad would have liked us to. There are so many shows that remind me of her and my brother growing up. Eva and I would always imitate commercials. We would find commercials so funny or so stupid that we would imitate them, especially if they had a little song that went with them. We would stand together and just recite these commercials and laugh and laugh and think we were just so funny.

Barbara Cassidy   She would have been seven or eight when she first saw *The Wizard of Oz* on television; she loved that film. They played it once every year and the children just loved it. I remember at the elementary school, nature paths were installed and there were these white wood chips to outline the path. The children thought that was so neat, and Eva said, 'That's just like in *The Wizard of Oz – Follow the Yellow Brick Road*.'

Dan Cassidy   *The Wizard of Oz* movie to us children was the movie, the big thing. That was the most fantastic film we could watch. It involved a lot of creative ideas that we were not really used to seeing from watching *I Love Lucy*. When that movie came on, it would be an event. '*The Wizard of Oz* is on.' 'Whoa! What time? Oh Mom, can we watch it?'

Margret Cassidy   Eva really liked movies from the 1940s. Even though she participated, did all the social things, in some ways she was just her own person. Most kids weren't into Marlene Dietrich and Judy Garland and Greta Garbo, but Eva was. So I guess when it comes to *Over the Rainbow* it's just because of Judy Garland. It's just an old-fashioned movie but she liked the music because it was old-fashioned.

Eva's family's overriding memories of Eva at this time are happy and uncomplicated…

Hugh Cassidy   In elementary school she smiled all the time. She was just so happy – Miss Sunshine, they called her. When she smiled the people just melted. She was just a fun and happy kid, always drawing sketches, doing stuff, swinging on the monkey bars, running around; always a busy, happy fun-loving kid.

Margret Cassidy   Even when she was real little you noticed that she wasn't following the crowd. It's hard to describe, but you started to notice that she didn't do what the crowd was doing or think what they're thinking. So she was always unique. I just remember pictures and visions of her face and she'd almost always be smiling.

'…she didn't do what the crowd was doing

or think what they're thinking.

So she was always unique.'

Margret Cassidy

'I can't say I was really worried about her academic

problems because I knew that she had other gifts.

We all knew that she was going to be an artist.'

Hugh Cassidy

Ain't No Sunshine

Ruth Murphy We came to the United States from India in 1973. I was eleven when I came over. It was a culture shock because we were a fairly middle-class Indian family and grew up close to Washington DC in a very low-income area, which was fairly mixed at the time race-wise, but with lots of drug addicts, lots of alcohol issues, lots of car thefts – I was comfortable in that chaos of kids without both parents, a nutty kind of a world, drugs all over. You grew up sifting through the addicts on the steps in my neighbourhood, but Eva's home in Bowie was much more suburban. I guess we were coming from different worlds.

Ruth Murphy, who became Eva Cassidy's best friend during their three years at junior high, was well prepared for the social and racial mix of Robert Goddard Junior High in Lanham, a neighbourhood close to urban Washington DC.
Up to this point the Cassidy children had been largely immune to the politics of race in America, at a time – in the 1960s and early 1970s – when it dominated national life…

Dan Cassidy My mother was particularly anti-racist. She'd been in Germany and lived through the war. She instilled that upon us, that we were not to be racist and not to use certain words that we were picking up at that time. That carried through all us kids. There was a lot of racism around us and luckily we were able – having the guidance of the family, especially my Mom – to get through and see all of that.

We were from Bowie, which at that time was the tenth-richest city in the United States. We didn't have much money, but it was a high-income, very safe, residential, sleepy area of 40,000 people at that time. I would say most homeowners had some sort of office or government job. At that time desegregation was the new thing. You move white students to a school in a black or a lower-income neighbourhood, so instead of going to a school that was one mile away for junior high, we went seven miles away. It was called bussing: we were bussed to Robert Goddard Junior High.

Bussing, which was introduced in cities across the country in the late 1960s, was intended to racially integrate America's schools, and all three of the younger Cassidy children made the fifteen-minute journey to Robert Goddard daily. The transition was to be difficult for all of them, as they found themselves in a racial minority and an unfamiliar social environment, quite different from suburban Bowie…

Barbara Cassidy There was a new law in Maryland and children were bused into different neighbourhoods to make a more equal mix of different types of people. In elementary school she had friends, but then at Goddard it was a totally different group of people. She had a hard time coping; Margret and Danny did also. A lot of the children who went to the school showed very aggressive and hostile behaviour and Eva and the other two children had a very hard time dealing with that. It was a different socio-economic group of people; they felt they didn't fit in and were different.

Hugh Cassidy Junior high school was when this happy-go-lucky, fun-loving little girl no longer was a happy-go-lucky, fun-loving little girl. She changed dramatically and got a lot more serious in junior high school because the kids made fun of her. She was a blonde, blue-eyed kid going to a school that was largely black and it changed her. She was no longer coming home fun and happy any more. She just got picked on – not beaten up – but a victim of name-calling by tough kids, both black and white. To her credit though, she never became a hater or anything like that.

Ruth Murphy For Eva it was completely different, there were kids not paying attention, not minding their manners. She would take them as being nasty or cold towards her and she might have had some experiences with some of those kids, but I don't think they were deliberate. I think she was so sensitive and she wanted people to be nice to each other. She would feel hurt when they weren't. Eva had a tough time working through that. She was extremely disappointed at some of the harshness of the world.

Margret Cassidy I think kids know which ones to target. I think they just knew she was different. There were some mean and nasty kids in that school; it was just a tougher neighbourhood. They were tough kids who smoked cigarettes when they were twelve years old and hung out. So it was two different types of people and they got a kick out of making fun of us and all three of us went through that.

Dan Cassidy It was the toughest time for us. If she was doing a good art project, then someone would come flick paint on her painting and they'd say, 'You bitch.' It wasn't always racial because the white kids were also unpleasant. She wasn't used to anyone being mean to her in a peer group; this wrecked her; she couldn't deal with it. She often started crying and she didn't really know how to fight back. She'd get out of the way very quickly – she couldn't deal with confrontation. She didn't want to win any fights; winning wasn't in her vocabulary.

We all went to the same Junior High with Eva and it was the toughest few years of my life that's for sure. It caused emotional problems for me and Margret. Eva didn't want to be hurt; she didn't want to let herself be hurt by what other people thought of her. She became very self-conscious and protective of her own feelings. That was to last the rest of her life unfortunately. She was a changed person indeed.

'Her pictures were just at an amazing level. I'd watch her draw them and I'd get side-tracked because I'm watching her create these really neat drawings.'

Ruth Murphy

Hugh Cassidy Junior high school was the start of when reality set in, when you realise if you open too much of yourself with your innocence and your openness, there are people who will wound you. They are very important years and your sense of yourself is fragile. You're trying to find who you are and where you're going – more so probably than at any other time of your life. You're not a little kid any more and you're not a grown-up either and you don't know how to handle certain things. When you've got to go out into the wicked world, you've got to prove yourself and it can be a little bit of a let-down. I don't think she ever fully got out of that.

Eva also struggled with her schoolwork. She found her academic work uninspiring, although she retained her enthusiasm for art…

Barbara Cassidy She didn't enjoy that school like she did elementary school. She just did the homework because she had to, but didn't really put a lot of effort in it. But, then again, in art she outshone the rest of her classmates. In creative writing she was good, but math and the sciences were difficult for her and her grades were generally mediocre.

Hugh Cassidy I'm not saying she was frivolous, but she had little strength in the sciences or maths. It really got to her, so she just did what she could do well and on the other things squeezed by. It's like most of us; we do what comes easy and kind of squeeze through. I can't say I was really worried about her academic problems because I knew that she had other gifts. We all knew that she was going to be an artist. She was getting better all the time; it was something she did every day. We knew she wasn't going to be an intellectual.

Ruth Murphy We were twelve or thirteen; we were in science class. It was two to each little lab table and she was my partner. Here I am sitting next to a kid who is really not listening to what we were doing in the school; she was busy doing her art. Her pictures were just at an amazing level. I'd watch her draw them and I'd get side-tracked because I'm watching her create these really neat drawings. We had a great time in class, we laughed. We joked, we would write notes back and forth.

The teacher would say, 'Eva! Ruth!' and we'd look up, then Eva would go right back to her art-work. School wasn't really my top priority, but I wasn't a bad student. I mean I usually got the work done. She didn't always do the work. She'd be sitting there just creating, making caricatures of the teacher, of the class, of the topics we were studying and she had these beautiful illustrations that helped me understand it. So I guess she was really listening.

Eva's interest in music developed as she persevered with her guitar playing. She continued to devour her parents' record collection and took part in musical activities at her new school…

Ruth Murphy We had chorus together. My sister was in the chorus and Eva's sister, Margret, was in the chorus. So the four of us were all there in different sections. She was an alto; I was a soprano. So we had more time together in common. We also had folk group, which was something out of school hours where we'd meet and sing. Eva would get a lot of solos in that, and our teacher Miss Bush would play the guitar.

Celia Murphy was a grade above her sister Ruth at Robert Goddard. She first met Eva in the folk group…

Eva's Mona Lisa, drawn aged 12.

Celia Murphy The folk group was this little group that met after school and we did music together. There must have been maybe ten or twelve of us and it was just a bunch of students. One of the music teachers, Mrs Walters, chose songs that were either very folksy or very spiritual, stuff that people sang in the 1970s. I think what she taught us stuck with Eva, as it did with me.

We didn't talk too much about any one subject, except maybe about God. That was always in our conversations. I know that she was not part of any organised religion, but I knew that she believed in God. The idea that God is in everyone, that he has his hand in everything, and you should act appropriately or respectfully of that notion, was something that I think she started much sooner than I did.

Despite Eva's involvement in these musical projects, her isolation at school and sense that she was different deepened…

Dan Cassidy My mother is the most down-to-earth constant person in the whole family and she was concerned when she saw her child unhappy. As a mother she would say, 'What's bothering you, dear? Is it something you can talk about?' but Eva didn't come home saying, 'Mom something terrible happened.' It had to be pried out of Eva.

Margret Cassidy We really supported each other emotionally because sometimes we felt like we were all we had. My mother was always there, but she didn't go to that school, she didn't know what it was really like. So one way that Eva and I got closer as we got older was when other people were mean to us. We would always try to help each other by complimenting them or telling the other one that we loved each other. We always did that for each other, even into adulthood.

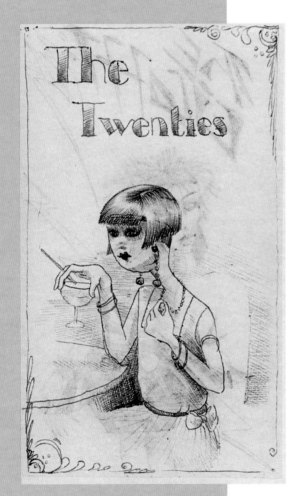

Hugh Cassidy Not everything was idyllic around here. I always got on the kids because neither Eva nor her brother did much around the house. I always felt 'Dammit, if I'm working three jobs and your mother's working one or two jobs you ought to be able to do a little something!' but every household faces this. They didn't want to wash dishes, didn't want to sweep the floor. A typical case is something's broken in the house and they continue to play in the yard and they know it's broken. I'd get angry because they wouldn't pick up that broken glass, or whatever it was, and I'd say, 'You saw that there and walked right around it and saved it for your mother and me to do?' But they were kids and they gradually learned. Somebody's got to be the heavy. I don't like to play that role, but if you don't call them to task and just let it go, I can tell you there'll be more of it. So my wife was Mrs Softy and I was the hard guy! That's just the way it was. Somebody's got to do it. It's a role.

Eva's solitary nature created problems in her friendship with Ruth, who was a more outgoing and popular teenager…

Ruth Murphy I guess I was in a popular group. Eva would tell me I was in a popular group. It created conflicts because she wouldn't share a part of that world with me, so I had to do things just with Eva. We'd go to movies, just Eva and myself. We'd just do kind of solitary things. We'd do projects together, take walks, go on bike rides or we'd go to museums. I saw a fun side, one that would burst into song, and was absolutely delightful to be with. Very clever, funny. It was not your run-of-the-mill humour and, once you got in tune with all that stuff, it was exciting. Eva chose people. She was very specific with whom she chose to share part of herself. She'd need to feel very safe. Every year you get a yearbook and she wrote in mine something about, 'You were the only one, the only friend who understood me, you are the only friend I had this year,' and she drew this beautiful picture of this Indian queen – looked Egyptian, but it was Eva's rendition of an Indian – which I thought was really sweet. You give her this yearbook to sign and, all of a sudden, she hands it back with this neat picture.

Eva's and Dan's musical interests were encouraged by their father…

Dan Cassidy My Dad was the type, who after realising that we were into music, would point out anything of relevance to us. If he heard a good singer on a record, he would bring home the record for Eva. He brought home a record called *Linda Ronstadt: A Retrospective*, which was basically her best stuff up to then. That would have been Eva's big influence. Absolutely. The first top singer Eva really took to.

It was around 1976 and Dad started getting into this country rock, bluegrass-type movement and he took up the mandolin. So having played mandolin, now he was learning a few fiddle tunes that we could play together and Eva naturally would accompany us. One time my Dad took us to this really, really big bluegrass festival and Eva was hearing a lot of harmony singing and was influenced by country rock singing.

The *Rumours* album by Fleetwood Mac had tinges of country rock. That was an influential record, so, Eva's first style of singing, apart from folk tunes or the odd pop tune, was definitely a repertoire of country rock. Her big number around that time was *Desperado* by the Eagles. She sang that beautifully and included it in her repertoire to the end of her career. And Dad introduced her to Emmylou Harris and she loved that and listened to it.

Ruth Murphy She was into so many different things, even in junior high school – like Ella Fitzgerald – she introduced me to Ella Fitzgerald. She would use vibrato, stuff that I didn't even know and I learned through Eva. She would pay attention to voices. She was extremely tuned to the voices and instruments. She knew her stuff; she knew her jazz; she knew her blues singers. That's very unusual for eleven or twelve year olds. That part was really cool; she taught me a lot of that.

Hugh, noticing the developing musical talents of his two children, took a step which was to have a huge influence on both of their lives…

Dan Cassidy Dad's aim was to turn us into professionals as kids, almost as a gimmick. His dream was to get us into playing professionally. He got on the bass, because he said that has to be tight and he was a very good bass player. After we had the nucleus of us three playing tight and our repertoire, we would audition other musicians to play lead guitar and drums.

Dad pushed us to reach a level beyond our abilities, Eva and myself. I seemed to be playing at a much higher level right away. We were pushed, but we rose to the challenge. None of us said, 'I don't want to do this, I'm quitting.' I was amazed that my Dad put so much energy into it. He'd won his world championship and now he had time for us. It was great. This was probably the most formative thing we had ever done. To rehearse a repertoire and actually go out and play and do a professional gig at that age was pretty heavy stuff.

'Eva chose people. She was very specific with whom she chose to share part of herself. She'd need to feel very safe.'

Ruth Murply

Ruth Murphy Eva loved the fact that she got to do music; she learned a lot about music from the family band. Hugh wanted to be a perfectionist about a lot of things and I don't think he meant any harm by offering what he would probably have thought were helpful hints. But the way Eva viewed the world, it was very harsh criticism. Could be that she learned to have such high goals and aspirations based on Hugh's prompting.

Dan Cassidy We were going through adolescence, so Eva and I weren't always friendly; and it was tough, but I do remember Dad pointed out to Eva, 'You've got to learn vibrato when you're singing. That can make or break a singer. Too much is awful, not enough can be boring.' He pushed her to learn vibrato. I don't know how he knew so much about music to teach us all this stuff. This is the early formative training that would shape the way she went about things for the remainder of her life.

For Eva, Dad was a key figure, absolutely. If there ever was one, he was it. And having had all this, not pressure but *encouragement*, we could take that on our own path, because the band didn't last very long at all.

The family band's short life was related, in part at least, to their first public performance…

Dan Cassidy We did our first gig at the Fleet Reserve Club in Annapolis, and Eva was very nervous and self-conscious and she tripped over the microphone lead, which knocked the mike stand over. It came crashing to the floor, making a hell of a racket, and she was in tears. Not a really good start. I hope that it didn't have any long-running effect on her enthusiasm for live performance; but if anything did, it was that. This was her first time playing in front of an audience.

Barbara Cassidy She must have been thirteen or fourteen at the time and to her that was just devastating – she was such a perfectionist all the time – that this should have happened to her.

Hugh Cassidy When she dropped the microphone, she was in tears. She just lost control of it. But she did not run away. She looked at me and I said, 'Go ahead and pick up the microphone.' So she made it through the song and got control of herself and the rest of the evening went smoothly. But that's not a typical reaction. If you drop the mike, you drop the mike. Maybe it was too soon for her to be on stage, but it wasn't as if she hadn't performed before. Since she was nine or ten, every Christmas, Easter and Thanksgiving we'd do something, but that was very safe. I don't think we played much after that, as a matter of fact; but that was natural. You don't want to be with your father, but I thought it was good training for her.

Eva's sensitive nature and problems at school coincided with the onset of puberty. At this time her parents sensed a growing distance from Eva…

Barbara Cassidy I think at fourteen or fifteen she withdrew a little bit and she did a lot of art-work but kept quite a bit to herself. At that time, she'd be in her room often, creating, playing music, drawing. The teen years must have been difficult for her. She was a little rebellious; teenage stages they all go through. Adolescence can be difficult for the teenager and the parents, and I think sometimes Hugh and Eva avoided each other to avoid conflict.

Hugh Cassidy Well, she no longer related to me as her Dad. You're too old for horsy games, naturally. I mean she would hang with kids of her age. That's the time when she started pulling away, and it's to be expected. She still followed her pursuits but there was a noticeable change. Probably that was just puberty. The separation was more severe than I would have liked, but I understand that's pretty par for the course.

The odd thing is that we are programmed to have children when we are in our twenties, but we're not given the wisdom to know how to handle those children. While you physically can have children, you don't have the wisdom. You're learning to be a parent and I told them this, too: I said, 'We're learning to be parents while you're learning to be adults, so cut us some slack here like we cut you some slack.' People having children in their twenties and thirties are still finding themselves and I was still hunting for myself. Perhaps my wife was settled down a little, but I know I wasn't.

While they are learning to be an adult, you're learning to be a father and so we both make mistakes along the way. You raise them in the way your mother and father did when they were in their twenties. So we're perpetuating it; it's kids having kids is what it amounts to. There's bound to be some friction and it happens.

Dan Cassidy Eva and Dad were very similar. Like magnets they either got along or didn't. We weren't a very close family any more, that's for sure. Maybe it was natural.

**A positive by-product of Eva's withdrawal during adolescence was the time
she spent concentrating on developing her musical talents and studying the singers
and songs that were to influence her future musical direction…**

Dan Cassidy She didn't really flit around enlightening us with her newly found singing projects. This was something she did on her own. She would definitely go in her room to

'I think at fourteen, fifteen she withdrew a little bit and she did a lot of art-work but kept quite a bit to herself. At that time, she'd be in her room often, creating, playing music, drawing. The teen years must have been difficult for her.'

Barbara Cassidy

work on her music. She had the smallest room of all the children. I don't know why that was. It was like a little hideaway, a very small room. And, of course, she would practise. My Dad said if you can practise half-an-hour a day you're gonna really show some progress.

Hugh Cassidy She would study Aretha Franklin, Sarah Vaughan, Ella Fitzgerald and Joan Baez and all these folks. It's a different thing: just listening casually to them as compared with studying them. So she knew their nuances and every little thing about them. She got up in that room there and listened to how they made a vocal lick and imitated it. She was up in that room for hours with the door closed, and I could hear music going on in there, but it was nothing that you could distinguish. I knew she was working at her craft. Eva went for her passion.

She learned the vibrato from Joan Baez. I agreed with her that there were few better people from whom she could learn that. Eva got up in her room and kept practising until she got her vibrato. I remember the day when she came down and she said, 'I got it!' I said, 'What'd you get?' She said, 'I got the vibrato.' I said, 'Let me hear it,' and she had it. She didn't have to force it; it was there. I hear many singers who are very good, but they lack that vibrato, that finishing touch. She had that.

Dan Cassidy On TV, which we watched tons of, there were commercials all the time and for a short time there was a woman singing jingles who had a beautiful singing voice. She sang a *Three Musketeers* candy bar commercial in nineteen-seventy-something. And my Dad once pointed out, 'Doesn't she have a beautiful voice?' Eva said, 'Yes,' and then we'd recognise this lady singing on another commercial. 'Hey, that's the same lady!'

This lady was good; this lady was absolutely fantastic. I'm talking about a white singing voice. She sang better than Joan Baez, Judy Collins, Buffy Sainte-Marie, or any of those people. I actually believe that Eva's whole approach to developing her own singing voice was based on this mystery woman. This lady sounded more like Eva sounded later – like she was to sound later – than anyone.

Kids can pick up information, even in the subconscious, that will last the rest of their lives, that will shape the way they go about approaching what they do. No one else is going to mention it because they weren't there and they weren't sitting on the sofa when we heard this lady sing. I don't attribute Eva's singing talent to her in any way, but she must have liked that style of singing, because I hear it again and again and again.

Although the family band had come to a premature end,
the desire to perform remained strong in Eva…

Dan Cassidy It was a very private thing. We'd come home from school and Eva would say, 'Do you want to play?' She had kept in her repertoire some of the tunes that Dad had showed her, a lot of tunes she liked. So I became her musical partner and we got a repertoire.

She was getting pretty good on guitar. She knew how to finger-pick pretty well. I think she was influenced by Paul Simon's acoustic guitar playing for sure. I switched to bass guitar and we clicked right away. We sounded great and there was a group called Kansas who had a song called *Dust in the Wind* with a violin. Immediately we said, 'Let's learn it.' She could finger-pick it beautifully; that was our big tune.

We were fans of *The Little Rascals*. Eva and I thought that was the best children's show ever put on TV. There was a wonderful episode where the whole gang somehow breaks into this wealthy home and they just go bananas because they've never been in a wealthy home and don't know what this stuff around them is. One of the characters, Mary, had a little brother and she led him because he was very small. She kept saying, as they were approaching this house and picking the lock and going in, 'Whatever you do, don't show your ignorance.' Eva just thought that was absolutely outrageous.

Once Dad took us to one of his regular gigs and let Eva sing a tune and let me play a tune. He took us to the Trojan Horse Room in the Holiday Inn for the ritzy people. We, as kids, thought it reeked of money and moneyed people, which we didn't really know too much about. Eva leaned over and said, 'Whatever you do, Dan, don't show your ignorance.' And that became our biggest, longest-running joke and catch-phrase.

Eva's eldest sister Anette, who had left home when Eva was eleven, recalls meeting up with her sister again and hearing her perform with Dan…

Anette Cassidy I remember her being a child and then when Mom and Dan came to visit me in Florida. I had moved there and lived there for several years. I guess they were teenagers by then. She'd gone from being a little girl to a young lady. She was very much Eva, very shy and very quiet and humble.

And that's the first time I really heard Eva sing and play the guitar and Dan play the fiddle. It just blew me away. I couldn't believe how good they had gotten. And they did this one tune, *Desperado*, which at the time I'd never heard before. It was the first time I ever heard the song when they did it, and I just got chills all over – the hair stood up on my arms – and to this day, I can still remember that feeling.

Eva's days at Robert Goddard were drawing to a close and the prospect of senior high school brought with it the chance for Eva and Dan to develop as musicians…

Dan Cassidy At that time my Dad pulled us both aside and said, 'Y'all need to get with some good musicians your own age,' and we said, 'Well, we don't really know anyone.' And he kept saying over and over, 'Wait till you get into high school; you're going to meet players better than you, and you're going to rise to the occasion.' And how he knew that I'll never know – because that's exactly what happened.

'She was just doing her thing on stage —

this little blonde girl singing her butt off up there with Dan —

strumming a twelve-string guitar while he played violin.'

Larry Melton

How Can I Keep From Singing?

OPPOSITE Eva at Larry Melton's, 1984, aged 21.

Dan Cassidy It was just like high school films. There are these spoiled people called jocks. They were on the football team and got all the girls. Then there were preps, who were upwardly mobile, well-dressed, academic, thinking they were very beautiful and important. There were people of dubious character, smoking dubious substances, called 'freak' or 'heads', and then there were the nerds with thick-framed glasses.

The jocks and the preps would intermingle, but the freaks and the jocks were enemies; and, of course, the preps looked down on the freaks as complete gutter trash. Cheerleaders went with the football players; that was a given. If a cheerleader went with a freak, it would be the most outrageous thing. She'd be kicked off the squad. It would be sacrilege. If you didn't fit into those categories it was very unusual. There was a lot of social peer pressure to be one or the other.

Eva was an 'I don't know what I'm going to be'.

It was into this environment that Eva moved when, in the autumn of 1978, she arrived at senior high school close to her home in Bowie. The challenges for a sensitive teenager like Eva were different from those she had experienced at Robert Goddard, but were nevertheless real and difficult…

Margret Cassidy Bowie High was about eighty per cent jock and cheerleader types and Eva and Dan and I did not fit that category whatsoever. I never went to any of my proms; Eva never even wanted to get her yearbook picture taken. We weren't into the pep

rally and homecoming, and Bowie High was very into appearances and old-fashioned school spirit. We just tuned out of that. We didn't go to football games and do all that stuff. We didn't want to be part of that; but even if we had, we weren't accepted.
We associated with a chosen few. We didn't want to be in a crowd of people that we didn't know and couldn't relate to. We wanted to be with people that we had something in common with, that really liked us and that we knew liked us. The 'chosen few', whoever they may be.

For Eva these 'chosen few' were drawn from the school's musical fraternity. One of its leading lights was a talented musician from Bowie called Ned Judy…

Ned Judy There were one thousand people in my graduating class, and it was very much sports-oriented. If you weren't in that clique, you had to find something else. So we found music and there was actually quite a large music scene. There were probably a dozen bands in our high school that could play fully orchestrated songs.

Dan Cassidy Eva and I performed *Dust in the Wind*, and maybe a couple of tunes by Neil Young and maybe a Janis Joplin, in the basement of the Bowie Library, where they had rock jams. We just did a few tunes and there were the musicians – at least half the musicians that would be significant – that we would later play with in bands.

Chesapeake Bay.

One of those at this early performance was Larry Melton, a bass player who would remain a friend and collaborator throughout Eva's life…

Larry Melton I saw her perform at the Bowie Library. This was right when I started playing. I must have been fourteen or fifteen, and I remember seeing Dan and Eva up there doing Kansas's *Dust in the Wind*. She was just doing her thing on stage – this little blonde girl singing her butt off up there with Dan – strumming a twelve-string guitar while he played violin. I was pretty floored and made a mental note, 'Wow, keep an eye on her; she's good!'

Eva subsequently joined Dan in a number of short-lived bands, performing material entirely different from the music she would later choose and record…

Dan Cassidy Any band I joined, I more or less invited Eva too. I introduced Eva to the concept of being in a band. I was in one that was called Night Wing, a heavy-rock band. We did heavy, heavy metal like *Iron Man* and *Paranoid* by Black Sabbath, but she did it nonetheless.

She had long straight hair and dirty jeans. Rock 'n' roll was a huge, huge influence. She discovered a band called Heart, which was the Wilson sisters, Anne and Nancy. Finally she'd found a group, a commercial group, that she could relate to: Anne Wilson was a real rock 'n' roll singer. Eva could sound just like her immediately; and Nancy Wilson played a very good guitar, so Eva had a role model in two people in the same band.

With Dan in Stonehenge, their high school rock group, 1982.

I formed another band with a friend of mine, a guitarist named Dave Lourim. We were called Blue Wind. We did one gig at the Sacred Heart church and Eva got to do all these Heart tunes, like *Crazy On You* and *Barracuda*. She sang the daylights out of these songs and she was playing the rhythm guitar, keeping right up. Some drunk guy kept asking us to do *Like a Rolling Stone* and had to be escorted out by the priest. So that didn't work, but we had done a professional gig.

Ned Judy I met Eva through music. I saw her playing with her brother Dan and a couple of other rock bands at dances around town and showcases. Our high school let us put on showcases once or twice a year. They called them Coffee Houses. I knew her through that and I saw her play. I was blown away because she sounded really mature. She sounded like a woman and that's how Eva was. I'd never heard anyone my age sing like that before. I knew she was the best person I'd heard up to that point.

Dan Cassidy Rock was a way for her to fit in with her social peer group. And, when
they found out that she could sing and they found out she was a brilliant artist,
she had a following – a recognition of being someone who was extraordinary and
talented, but one of them.

**The impression Eva made with these early performances gave her an introduction
to a group of friends with whom she would remain close all her life – friends who had an
important influence on the development of her talent. The group was brought together
by their mutual devotion to the work of the English progressive rock band, Yes, whose
complex arrangements they were devoted to replicating…**

Dan Cassidy This fellow named Ned Judy was the very best musician in the school,
far and away, light years ahead of the pack. He decided to put this band together to play
this grandiose piece by Yes called *Close to the Edge* – a 20-minute long anthem. It was
loud rock with incredible vocal harmonies.

Larry Melton First it was the drummer, Mark Merella, myself on bass and Dave
Lourim, the guitar player, who had a little jam at Mark's house. I knew Ned a little and
Dave knew Eva a little bit, so somehow we just pieced it together.

Ned Judy I think her boyfriend at the time, a guy named Thurston, dropped her off
and picked her up afterwards and she was a mystery to us. She was this amazing singer
who was gracing us with her voice. Everyone in the room felt like that.
I remember the deal we made before our first gig. It was like – in order to get me we have
to play *Close to the Edge* by Yes, because there's a big keyboard fest, and Eva has to do a
Janis Joplin song and Larry's going to want to do a Jeff Beck piece. And that was a big
compromise. She was coming out of a rock, blues background. So we knew she was into
that stuff and we even did some Heart songs and other things she was into.

Larry Melton The music of Yes had something for all of us – vocal harmonies and lush
instrumental sections.

**The new band chose the suitably 'progressive' name of Stonehenge and booked
themselves a concert at one of the high school's Coffee House showcases…**

Dan Cassidy Stonehenge was the most significant band I think Eva was ever in. This
was *the* band, the best players you could ask for. They were playing better than we could
imagine any kids at this age playing. I was a little jealous that she got in this wonderful
band. They performed at the Coffee House. I was in the second row watching and Eva
sang a tune called *Turtle Blues* by Janis Joplin.
She was so nervous before this concert, taking a shot of Canadian whiskey to get up
the courage. She got up there and sang the hell out of this song. I mean,
really let herself go and the whole audience was shouting before the song was over.
I mean, the effect she had – like she was a badass chick up there all of a sudden, singing

the blues. She sang fantastic; she really had it; she was confident. Everyone thought it was wonderful.

Larry Melton She performed great. In fact, she had her own little cheering section at our first gig. The place came alive. When she started *Turtle Blues* her little clique of friends were cheering, 'Eva, yeah!' and I think that probably helped her, having a little support system there. The place lit up when she started singing that blues. You hear the voice and you're like, 'Whoah she's really belting it out.' I think she was sitting down, strumming the guitar and singing, just belting out this blues.

Eva's publicity poster for her group Stonehenge, 1982.

Dan Cassidy Then came *Close to the Edge* and she got through the whole thing and had the harmonies going. We were mesmerised. I would have liked to see another band have a girl at that age get through the first three minutes. But Eva played it all down. Whatever Eva did she'd play it down and say, 'Oh, that wasn't that good.' She was very critical of anything she did and that's how she reached – in my opinion – this incredible level of singing.

Eva arranged for Dan to join Stonehenge on violin and the band began rehearsals in the garage of drummer Mark Merella's home…

Ned Judy She broke up with this Thurston guy pretty soon and I started driving her to rehearsal. I'd pick up Dan and Eva and they wouldn't say a word the whole way to rehearsal. Silence. It was the most awkward time. And then afterwards, neither one would ever say a word. Give them a ride home and get, 'Turn left at the sign,' and that was it. I couldn't shut them up a couple of years after that; but at first, I don't know if they were terrified or what.

Larry Melton They were very new to us, Dan and Eva. They were kind of a team when they joined the band. Then basically it was rehearsal and hanging out afterwards. That was our social scene. People would come over and watch our rehearsals and come to our gigs. So we had our own little following and own little clique. As well as a band, we were a group of friends, too.

'I didn't know her in junior high but she told me that she felt that she was picked on. She said she felt she was like Charlie Brown, the Peanuts character, and that she'd never do anything right and she'd get picked on all the time.'

Ned Judy

The time spent in the Merella garage was to mark a significant change for Eva: for the first time since her elementary school days she was able, gradually, to find a group of friends with whom she could relax and break through her shyness…

Mark Merella We turned our parents' garage into our little rehearsal space and we'd be there like five, six nights a week. We would just play for a couple of hours and then we'd just hang out and socialise. It turned into a kind of social scene in a way, because we'd rehearse there, and sometimes friends would stop by to listen. My parents liked the fact that I wasn't out on the streets or whatever.

Ned Judy We started to warm up to each other; it was kind of a rite of passage for us. We didn't have anything else for us in that town, so we added our own spice. We started hanging out, literally every night, and became best friends as a group. We went camping together, went to the beach together, hung out in the woods, went to movies.
And I think that little family group we had opened her up a little. I didn't know her in Junior High but she told me that she felt that she was picked on. She said she felt she was like Charlie Brown, the *Peanuts* character, and that she'd never do anything right. She was definitely isolated and that's what she told me, and as she was telling me, I could see it had had an effect on her.

Larry Melton On the surface she was shy, but when she let you in, when you got to know her, she was anything but shy, I can tell you that. She was animated; she was very funny; she loved to do impressions. She could imitate singers and do accents, make up words. Like she would do a fake German thing or she'd just piece together words from hearing her mother speak. So it took a while to break through; but once you did, she was very open and animated. She certainly was shy performing, but as a friend it was the opposite; the walls were down; there was no more real shyness.

Hugh Cassidy People liked Eva because she still had some of that sunshine left and they knew she was talented. She could draw pictures of little things and make people laugh. She used to joke and laugh and do imitations and things. She never would do imitations for me, but I have it on good authority that she could imitate Barbra Streisand and do all the facial things. She could imitate Judy Garland and get it right on centre. You name the popular singers of the day, the women singers, and she could do them all. Once in a while I'd catch her when she didn't know I was around and I'd hear her doing them and I'd think, 'Gee, this is pretty good.'

Barbara Cassidy Monica Merella, now Monica Steiner, was Mark's younger sister by nine years. She relished Eva's attention when the band was playing at Mark Merella's house. Eva introduced young Monica to some of her favourite outdoor haunts. Monica remembers Eva's childlike wonder towards all living things – faces in clouds, sunlight filtering through foliage. She continues to view life through Eva's way of 'seeing'.

Stonehenge 1984.
(from left) Ned Judy,
Larry Melton, Eva
Cassidy, Dan Cassidy,
Todd Bauchspies.

For a short time at high school Eva and Mark were boyfriend and girlfriend. Mark was impressed by Eva's talent and intrigued by her personality…

Mark Merella One of her friends picked up that I liked her and I think the word got back to Eva, as it works in high school. We just started seeing each other after that. I liked her personality because she had this kind of air of mystery about her – like you could never quite tell what was on her mind. To me that was attractive. After we broke up we stayed friends, really good friends, because I think we just realised that the greater sum of the equation was being friends. I mean, at that age you're going through so many changes that it's almost inevitable that you're going to go your separate ways, so, when the romance thing broke off, it was much more important to stay friends. I'm really happy that was the case, because we had a lot of good times after that.

All her life Eva had some difficulty with live performance. From her days in Stonehenge on, there was a persistent tension between her desire to perform and express herself and a reluctance to step into the limelight…

Ned Judy She was very shy, wouldn't really look at the audience. Eva always wore things that would cover her body. She was a very beautiful woman, but she was not very much into exploitation of women, especially bodies. So she wore very baggy clothes, always a long flannel shirt that went down half-way to her knees. She was not out-going, not a

front person during Stonehenge and as long as I knew her. She would just leave if she wasn't needed on stage. She didn't want to be an icon or ornament.
The keyboards, the violin, her voice and all of our voices ran through the same sound system, so she had to sing pretty loud. But then we'd each do a solo. Eva would come out with her guitar and sing *Georgia on my Mind* – something a little out of character for the band, and it would just blow people away. It wasn't her mannerisms and her stage presence. It was just purely her voice. People screamed her name.

The stage dynamics of a loud high-school rock-and-roll band were difficult for Eva, who was always more comfortable performing ballads…

Barbara Cassidy She joined in, but very often she didn't like the material. The musicians were always too loud and she had to scream at the top of her voice just to be heard. She was the only female, so she always felt she had to struggle with those guys. She didn't like rock music that much, but she realised that it gave her a chance to perform.

Hugh Cassidy She sang her guts out, her lungs out, and I kept telling her: 'You gotta get with a group that doesn't make you scream so much.' In later years she admitted that she was really having to scream to get over the drums and the horns and all the noise.
At the time she was accepted and she was a singer and she liked it, even though I'd look at it and say, 'Gee, how can you handle that?'

Eva and Dan performing with Stonehenge, 14th May 1982 at P.G. Community College.

Before the baggy clothes.

I wasn't into that screechy metallic fusion stuff. That wasn't me, and eventually it proved it wasn't her either, but she was socially accepted. These guys were friends of hers and they were peers. She had some fun and got some recognition, too. People knew who she was.

Despite the acceptance and admiration Eva received as a consequence of Stonehenge, she continued to feel isolated at school…

Margret Cassidy Eva didn't fit the norm of what your typical Bowie girl should look like. She told me one time that when she was just walking down the hallway there were these jock guys all lined up in the hallway and she walked by and they didn't know her or know anything about her, but she said they spat at her. I was so angry when she told me that, really, really angry.

Dan Cassidy She didn't have a good self-image. I saw a piece of art-work she had done. She drew a picture of a pig crying drops of blood and I went 'eeeugh', because I'd never seen anything like that eerie picture. And, my being the ignorant younger brother, I said, 'Why did you draw that? What is this supposed to be?' She said, 'That's me.' I said, 'Really, come on, that's not you.' She said, 'Yes it is.' I said, 'Come on, that's a pig crying drops of blood,' and she said, 'That's just how I feel sometimes.' And that was the first time I really got a little concerned about her self-image, because it was her own self-caricature. That's what she claimed to me. She would have been around seventeen at this time and she was very sensitive.

Margret Cassidy One thing that Eva and I had especially was a little game. I'd say, 'Eva, you're so pretty,' and she'd say, 'No, you're so pretty,' and then I'd say, 'You're the prettiest,' and then she'd say, 'No, you're the prettiest.' It sounds silly, but we just always told each other things to make each other feel better – like from all the negative input we got from other people.

'So she wore very baggy clothes, always a long flannel shirt

that went down half-way to her knees.

She was not out-going, not a front person during Stonehenge

and as long as I knew her.' Ned Judy

Dan Cassidy She was known for her art. Even some of the jocks knew Eva and saw her at the Coffee House and knew Stonehenge was far and away the best band in the school. She had many young ladies wanting to be her, believe it or not – because if you had talent, you were somebody.

Mark Merella She had some recognition. She was voted 'most talented' and the picture they had in the school newspaper wasn't even her yearbook picture.
It was a picture of her at one of those talent shows, just her and her guitar. Everyone else, they had their yearbook picture, so it was kind of like she was recognised, but still the outsider.

In 1981 Eva graduated from Bowie High School and began working with her sister Anette, who had returned to the area, as a 'hot walker' at Bowie's horse racing track…

Anette Cassidy We worked for the same trainer for a while. He was an old Southern gentleman, really getting on in years. He didn't like driving, so whenever he could, he would get somebody else to drive his big long Cadillac, and here's Eva sitting behind the wheel. She was so tiny. They were out one day and a small animal ran into the road, a squirrel or a rabbit, and she was not going to hit an animal. So she ran down the brakes and almost took the car into the ditch to avoid it. He just couldn't believe it had happened, I think he was angry to begin with, and then, as he got to see the kind of person that she was, he realised that was just Eva.

Ned Judy The people at the race track weren't as sensitive as she was. I mean she was this ultra-sensitive person who wouldn't hurt a flea. They were obviously trying to trap rats and exterminate the rats, and she was being devious and letting them free from the traps and getting into trouble for it. I think she got caught, but I'm not sure about that. But then one day, this guy caught a rat and killed it right in front of her, just to spite her. It was really cruel what he did and she came home crying that day. Because she had been setting the rats free, he wanted to make the point and really terrorise her. And he did, and she quit.

'We worked for the same trainer for a while. He was an old Southern gentleman, really getting on in years. He didn't like driving, so whenever he could, he would get somebody else to drive his big long Cadillac, and here's Eva sitting behind the wheel. She was so tiny.

They were out one day and a small animal ran into the road, a squirrel or a rabbit, and she was not going to hit an animal.

So she ran down the brakes and almost took the car into the ditch to avoid it.' Anette Cassidy

MARYLAND
LEARNER'S PERMIT

C-230-238-585-088
CONTROL NO.   SP. CODE RESTR.   CLASS
L734119   D
HGT.   WGT.   SEX   LIC. TYPE
5-02   110   F   N
EXPIRES   BIRTH DATE
05/05/82   02/02/63
SIGNATURE
Eva Cassidy

EVA MARIE CASSIDY
6604 HIGH BRIDGE RD
BOWIE   PG MD 20715

Ned Judy, more than any other person in Eva's life at this time, came to understand the connection between her sensitivity and her artistic talents. The two had grown close and the turning point in their relationship came on Ned's ninteenth birthday...

Ned Judy She gave me a painting for my birthday that blew me away. It's a picture of me up in the mountains playing a piano. It was perfect for me. If she could have painted the perfect picture for me, it was that. I mean, she read into my heart and mind and knew what I wanted to see. That's what impressed me; it was the heart behind it. It wasn't the painting itself; it was her doing it for me. I didn't have a choice after that. She gave me that, and shortly after that, things happened between us.

I think that her artistry came out because she could perceive things so well. When we walked through the woods together she would say, 'Look at the face on that tree,' or, 'Look at that grumpy tree.' Some people walk through the woods and don't see anything, but she saw a face on every tree or cloud.

> 'She gave me a painting for my birthday that blew me away. It's a picture of me up in the mountains playing a piano. It was perfect for me. If she could have painted the perfect picture for me, it was that. I mean, she read into my heart and mind and knew what I wanted to see. That's what impressed me; it was the heart behind it.' Ned Judy

It was the same thing with her music. She could sense emotion and she could reflect it back. She could make people cry just by cracking her voice a little or she could make them laugh by doing an Ethel Merman impression. She was really subtle; she could really tweak people's emotions. Always, ever since the first time I saw her sing, she could do that. I don't know if she was conscious of it, it might have just been second nature. She would get the feedback from the audience. When people were really engaging with her, she would definitely play with their emotions, but she wouldn't reflect it in her mannerisms or stage presence. She was just perfectly still, putting everything she had into her voice and her guitar.

The musical education Eva received from her father was to have a profound influence on her musical life thereafter. She first drew upon the songbook of American standards he had taught her, in a project conceived by her brother Dan...

Dan Cassidy We had a following, of course, of freaks who dug progressive rock. But the first summer into this Stonehenge thing I needed money; Ned needed money; Eva needed

'At this time Eva really started practising singing and listening to black R'n'B singers, which was to be very important. Her biggest influences were Stevie Wonder, Aretha Franklin, Ray Charles, early James Brown — she loved that — and Phoebe Snow.'

Dan Cassidy

money. We knew all these old-fashioned tunes, standards from the 1930s and 1940s, and said, 'Hey, let's form a money-making band and get gigs and do weddings.'

Ned Judy They brought Hugh's songbook over one night and we looked at it and thought, 'We can do this. Let's get our own band together and start making some money, be commercial, try the other side, see if we can be professional musicians.' We did stuff out of her father's book of American standards: *Autumn Leaves, Mack the Knife, Georgia on my Mind.*

Dan Cassidy I named the band Easy Street – an easy way to make money – and we signed up with the Washington Talent Agency. We were a four-piece band and we were going out doing gigs under contract all over the Washington DC area. We had to wear these horrible 1970s-ish light-blue, flared bellbottom tuxedos and Eva had to wear a dress and we did forty-something gigs, solid professional experience. We did a lot of tunes that were in my Dad's folder; and Eva knew those tunes, so she was a professional singer, doing professional gigs, at eighteen years old.

Ned Judy We did our very first gig at the Manassas Elks Lodge. It was a fraternal order, like the Masons or something. Eva was wearing an evening gown and looked really nice. She wasn't playing guitar a lot on some of the tunes, and when she would walk off the stage, these men would ask her to dance, and that was just not pleasant for her. She wouldn't dance. So she stayed on stage with us the entire gig, whether she was singing or not – hanging with the security of her band.

Dan Cassidy On the second gig some drunk guy insisted we play *Proud Mary*. We did it, and he then comes up five minutes later and goes, 'Play *Proud Mary*.' He was wasted. It was his party, his private party at a very posh country club in Potomac, Maryland, and we said, 'But we've just played it.' 'Play it again,' he said. Then his wife comes up and grabs him by the tie and says, 'Can't you play something this old fart can dance to?' And we just looked at each other thinking: 'Whoa, this is a rough little gig.' All of a sudden, Eva's playing for real grown-ups in real drinking situations. We had never heard anything like that.

Easy Street lasted less than a year, but gave Eva valuable experience in the realities of performing. It highlighted some of the recurring problems she faced later in her career…

Ned Judy One thing that happened almost all the time when we played Easy Street gigs is people would say, 'Smile, smile, come on, liven up.' That's the wrong thing to say to Eva, because it would just make her shut down more and more. I've heard dozens of people tell her, 'Smile.' And she was getting really into it. It wasn't that she was depressed; she was just very serious on stage. But people when they hire bands for parties or whatnot, they want to see people jumping around and being lively.

Eva at Ned Judy's, 1983.

Dan Cassidy In Easy Street her influence was Ella Fitzgerald. Ella was queen. She was the greatest to Eva at that time – the personification of swing female vocals. Eva picked that right up. Eva had a wonderful record of Ella live in Berlin from 1961. There was an incredible version of *How High the Moon* with an extended scat solo and she'd mimic all these instruments. I mean, Eva had never heard anyone sing on that level, doing those sorts of impersonations, just spontaneously on stage. Ella was God to Eva for a while – for quite some time her favourite singer.

At this time Eva really started practising singing and listening to black R 'n' B singers, which was to be very important. Her biggest influences were Stevie Wonder, Aretha Franklin, Ray Charles, early James Brown – she loved that – and Phoebe Snow.

Easy Street was not the only early professional experience Eva, Dan and others in Stonehenge gained. Eva took lead vocals one summer in a country banddressed in Roy Rogers costumes, playing for the crowds at the local theme park, Wild World…

Ned Judy Wild World was the first really steady income stream that I had, so it allowed me to buy a four-track recorder and a mixer and some effects. Eva loved it. She was coming over all the time and she immediately started over-dubbing her voice. She went into over-dub harmonies and did three- and four-part harmonies.

Right after I got the recording equipment, we recorded *The Rose*. That was just an experiment in vocal harmonisation. She wanted to do a piece like a three-part female and then a lead against three-part background harmonies. She came over with a kind of sketch of an idea that she wanted. I helped her a little bit, but it was basically her thing.

That was the first time she went into any kind of studio environment and actually did a demo tape. Before that, if you wanted to hear Eva, you had to hear her live. For the first time she could record herself. So that was the first real recording that I know that she did that sounded decent.

Some say Love, whoo, some say Love,
oooh oooh oooh some say Love,
Some say Love , whoo , some say love
ooh oooh oooh, some say love,
     ooh _____ ooh —
endless aching need.
but I say Love , ooh I say love
ooh ooh ooh ooh.
Its the heart ,   ooh, its the heart
ooh   ooh   ooh , yes its the heart
=|
Its the dream   ooh yes its the dream
ooh ooh ooh   yes its the dream,
      ooh _____ ooh who can not
seem to give,
Its the soul , ooh yes it the soul
ooh ooh ooh that never learns to live,

when the night , has been too lonely,
oooh   ooh.
  And you think, that love is only
  ooh ooh ooh lucky and the stong
    oooh _____ ooh, far beneath
the bitter snow _____
  that the seed , with the sun's love
  oooh ____ ooh _____
  in the spring becomes
    the rose _____

ABOVE Eva's lyrics
and arrangement for
The Rose. Eva played it
for the first time at work
during her lunch hour.

RIGHT Clowning around
with Ruth Murphy.

**Before she made this recording, Eva's friends and family knew she had
an impressive voice, but a career in music was not discussed as an option.
For Eva's mother *The Rose* changed all that…**

Barbara Cassidy When she played with those bands and she had to scream, I always
    sort of felt sorry for her and wondered just how long her vocal chords were going to last
    with all this screaming. To me it just wasn't pleasant to listen to, but then one time she
    put in this tape and it had her singing *The Rose*, the song Bette Midler had made famous,
    and it gave me goose bumps. There was this gorgeous ballad and it really blew me away.
    I started thinking, 'There is really something special going on.' That was when it dawned
    on me how beautiful her voice was. She had made a tape and played it for us and I knew
    there was something great. That was the moment I realised.
Isabel Bligh, Eva's aunt, really believed in Eva's talents right from the beginning.
    She was there for Eva's performances when hardly anyone else showed up. She gave
    Eva a lot of moral and also financial support. A great lady! Eva called her Patron Saint
    of the Arts.

**However, the difficulties of the Easy Street performances
sent Eva in a different direction – towards her art…**

Ned Judy Disney pours a lot of money into the California Institute of the Arts and they groom their animators there. They train them. Anyone who goes to Cal Arts for animation will probably work for Disney. I think Eva thought she would give animation a try, so she submitted a lot of pen-and-inks and character drawings. She assembled them into a portfolio and sent it off. They accepted her, but she applied too late for a scholarship. She was disappointed, but she was accepted – that was the big thing.

She was more concerned about being accepted than about actually going. Actually going was the most remote wish. Just being accepted by this prestigious school was enough, I think. It reassured her. She had this safe nest, not just at home, but of her buddies – us, Stonehenge and her friends that she had finally warmed up to and opened up to. She trusted people for once in her life. To abandon that and go to a whole new group of people was a big deal for her. She talked to me about her fear of leaving and going to the unknown.

She didn't have to decide. And I can't tell you what she would have done, but I think she was 50-50 at best, even if she'd had the money.

Barbara Cassidy She was just out of high school. I don't think it would have gone very well. She was not mature enough at this point to live by herself and also, at Walt Disney, you have to do what you're told: his style. I never really had any regrets about that.

The alternative for Eva was furthering her artistic education at a local college, but Prince George's Community College was to be a disappointment…

Ruth Murphy I remember I'd go to meet her there and give her a ride, catch up there at some point, and she would be very, very frustrated or exhausted from some of the art classes. One in particular where she just didn't think the instructor understood her and he was very critical of her work. Now I'm assuming this guy's just trying to help her grow, but she said he was very personal, like he was trying to change who she was. She would get hurt; she took it personally and she would go off and crawl into her shell and get angry with the world for being so imperfect. She ended up just dropping out of the college.

Barbara Cassidy She said, 'I'm not learning anything. The skills of the Old Masters are all getting lost,' and so she really had a tough time there and didn't pursue it any more. She had her own ideas; she wanted to do things her way and not listen to her instructor. That's Eva for you. She had a portfolio of stuff and her instructor wrote, 'Eva, you are good, but you could be great if you were only listening.' She probably should have accepted a little bit of what people were saying.

Eva's departure from art college led her back to music. She worked hard to lay the ground work for the performances and recordings to come…

Dan Cassidy She didn't have a direction – that was clear. She didn't have a career, but this gave her all the more time to be listening and practising. I remember there was a time when she bought an antique Fender amp and a microphone and finally could practise and sing with reverb. She was hooked on reverb. It made her sound better and it encouraged her to sing better than she would. So she was really practising a lot at that time.

Ned Judy From then on it was music. She started really practising a lot. Her guitar and her voice noticeably improved. Her intonation improved, her guitar accompaniment was becoming more imaginative, like she was taking time to work things out, polishing.

Eva won first prize for her 'New Guinea Chief' in a painting competition at Prince George's Community College.

Larry Melton I had saved up money and got a four-track cassette player. I barely knew how to work this new machine and Eva comes over with this gospel thing in mind. I think we did one or two vocals and then she wanted handclaps, but it had to sound like more than one person. So we did a couple of tracks of handclaps. The song was *Way Beyond the Blue* and the version showed up on Eva's album, *Time After Time*. The last cut on the album is the actual one I recorded. What you hear on the record is basically what happened in my bedroom. It was a surprise to me that it ended up on there.

In 1983 Dan Cassidy quit Stonehenge and the following year began four years of living and working as a musician in Europe. At the same time Stonehenge folded…

Ned Judy The band broke up at the same time as my relationship with Eva did. Everything kind of broke up at once. During the Stonehenge time she was like glued to the whole group. Over the course of my relationship with her, I was trying to push her, saying, 'You're a brilliant artist.' Gradually she became more independent and eventually I wasn't her security blanket any more. She didn't have to talk to me every day or else totally freak out. So we just grew up and matured. I don't know what actually happened in the end; it just fizzled out.

It was a little rocky after our relationship ended, of course; but I got over it, and she got over it. One night she came over to my house and she said she was ready to make a demo. This wasn't messing around, fooling around, experimenting – she really wanted to do a

Eva with Larry Melton, Bowie 1984.

demo. So we set up a couple of mikes and she just sang, to kind of archive her arrangements – so she could remember them – and I was blown away, sitting there with the headphones on, like, 'Wow!' It was amazing.

When she was twenty-two or twenty-three, she started taking arrangements seriously and so began stylising the songs. She realized she was a song stylist – that was her role – and she was going to go for it. She would just improvise over and over again and keep the best improvisation. It kept building and building and building, and after a couple of years she had full-fledged arrangements.

And that's when she first sang *Over the Rainbow*, same arrangement, same guitar. Not as polished, but the arrangement was as it is today. The arrangement was settled. I guess that was eight or ten years before she recorded it. She'd be sitting there in her room by herself, and she wouldn't have people to play off. She would just have the song to play off, and I think she reflects the words very well. She could put something new into *Over the Rainbow* because she's a creative genius. Some people can breathe new life into anything old.

Eva sent a copy of the recording to her brother in Europe…

Dan Cassidy Eva kept in touch now and again. She sent me a demo tape she'd made with Ned on a four-track cassette recorder. There were five or six songs and she sang her own harmonies. It included a song called *The Rose* that was done by Bette Midler. I was very impressed. She'd reached a new level after I'd been a year away. *Over the Rainbow* was on this demo; and it was her own arrangement, the exact arrangement that holds for her famous recording of it. You could see it better if you had moved away, if you hadn't heard her for a year. I thought, 'Wow, she's really getting good.'

'She was a feminist; she hated the exploitation

of women. That you have to wear sexy clothes

on stage really, really turned her off.'

Barbara Cassidy

People Get Ready

If Eva Cassidy's artistic vision had not been so securely set by the time she was in her mid-twenties in the mid-1980s, her story might have been very different. In 1984, her friend and former boyfriend, Ned Judy, left Bowie and established a successor group to Stonehenge…

Ned Judy I was in Baltimore studying composition and piano. I lived in a loft downtown, an old place with bricks, and we set up a theatre in there. We worked out of there. The band Characters Without Names came into being, doing more techno-pop kind of stuff – not really Eurythmics, but kind of similar to that – 1980s, drum machine, stuff like that. Eva liked Annie Lennox a lot because she's a really soulful singer. So, we started to get into that kind of thing and we were going to have a multi-media show. We were going to project Eva's art and animation and we had one piece, *A Star Passed By*, where she actually wrote some of the words. It was a ballad, a beautiful ballad. We recorded all the tunes; we had an album full of stuff.

I was graduating from school and getting the urge to get out. It would have been a perfect time to go to Los Angeles because Mark Merella and Larry Melton of Stonehenge were already there. Soon with me – half the band was in LA.

We said to Eva, 'Come with us, just go,' but she didn't want to do the techno Annie Lennox stuff we were doing in Characters Without Names. She was getting into *Over the Rainbow*

and she was determined to stick that out. A few years earlier she'd realised that was her role, song stylist, and she started getting away from original material. Eva didn't want to go.

After leaving art college Eva took a job at a plant nursery called Behnke's, where her mother worked. This job, which had been intended as a short-term measure while she decided on a permanent career, turned out to be the principal wage-paying job of Eva's life. The work Eva did at Behnke's was largely outdoors and involved heavy lifting. Most of her colleagues were men…

Hugh Cassidy She liked that idea of being able to handle heavy stuff like a guy. She never liked being patronised because she was a woman and hated the typical male-dominant, bullying, sneering type. They were loading a truck and some big truck driver was saying, 'Well, little Missy, you want a hand with that? Can I help you, little Missy?' and she just lit into him, cussed him down and let him have it. She wasn't going to take that. She was not a pugnacious individual, but she just did not take a put-down because she was a woman. I admired her for that. She stuck up for herself; that was good. I wish she had done that earlier on at junior high – just reached out and punched somebody in the nose.

Ruth Murphy She hated the conversations the guys would have, because women were always put down and the jokes were always a very poor portrayal of women. Eva was always into women's rights, even down to the nudity in movies. She really resented the fact that they showed

At Larry Melton's, 1984.

The Behnke Nurseries Company
BELTSVILLE, MD. 20705
937-1100
"KNOWN FOR QUALITY PLANTS"

women and didn't show men. She thought it should be fair, and we'd criticise movies based on that. She believed in equality for everybody, so Behnke's would have been difficult because it was predominantly male.

Barbara Cassidy She was a feminist; she hated the exploitation of women. That you have to wear sexy clothes on stage really, really turned her off. This started in her late teens and it stayed with her for the rest of her life. The way women are portrayed as sex symbols, or as pets even, really disturbed her.

Hugh Cassidy She always stuck up for the underdog. She was politically correct before it was politically correct to be politically correct, and any jokes, or anything that belittled in any way, no matter how innocuous, she would pick up on. Frankly it got to be a pain. Sometimes when you talked with Eva you had to walk on eggs; you had to be careful. It's uncomfortable being with a person who's not listening to what you're saying so much as picking up on if you say something derogatory about somebody else. In a way that's admirable and in a way it gets a little wearing, because we are human after all!

In the months before his departure for Los Angeles, Ned Judy did some work for a group called Method Actor, led by original Stonehenge guitar player David Lourim. Lourim also persuaded Eva to sing on the album and arranged for her vocals to be recorded at a studio in nearby Rockville, run by engineer and musician Chris Biondo, who was to play a significant role in her career…

Chris Biondo I was running a studio out of the basement of the house I was living in. I was engineering and I was trying to make a go of the band thing myself. I was playing in a group that had a female singer at the time and it was total crap; it had drum machines, synthesizers, that kind of stuff. Madonna was just getting going, so that's how far back it goes.
David Lourim called me and booked some time and we recorded a couple of his songs with no vocals one day. He said he was going to bring a singer over. He said, 'She's real good,' but I didn't believe him. I didn't expect very much.
The studio was in the basement and the door of the studio was around the back of the house. The guitar player walked in the door and I said, 'Where's the singer?' and he said, 'She's out there.' She was standing a couple of feet outside, her arms crossed, looking at the ground. I don't know if she was scared to come in but I looked at her and I said, 'Get in here!'

By the late 1980s Chris Biondo had worked with a diverse range of clients in his studio, including punk rock, rap and go-go groups, but the singer who appeared that day in early 1987 proved to be a unique challenge…

Chris Biondo Eventually she walked in and when you do what I do and strangers walk in all the time, what you do is try to lighten people up. I try to mess with people that I'm working with to get a feel for what they're like. I throw some comedy at them and see how they react and see how crude it can go. I think I made a real crude remark. The reaction I got was a grimace, like, 'Oh God, I've got to stay in here with this guy.' It worked for me for fifteen years to mess with people like that, but I don't think it really ever worked with Eva. I think she was pretty put off by me the first time I met her. I'm sure that she would really have preferred to have left immediately.

I put her in the vocal room and we started doing the background vocals for the choruses and she sang some very interesting harmonies. At first I thought she'd just gotten lucky and hit a note that she wasn't trying to hit. Then she sang the lead vocal, and I was thinking to myself, 'This is somebody who's better than anybody I'm working with right now.' It took me ten or fifteen seconds to realise that; it would have been faster if I hadn't thought that first note was a mistake.

She had the ability to hear harmonies in her head; she didn't have to work them out. It's not just singing the right note and pitch, but it's also singing with the lead vocal part, switching at the same time and holding the note at the end of the line the exact same way. She really had excellent short-term memory – somebody throws a bunch of notes and she sings it right back.

Chris Biondo was also struck by her personality…

Chris Biondo I thought she was very quiet, probably very conservative and naïve. In a lot of ways I was right about a lot of those things. I mean she just was very, very shy and very, very withdrawn into herself. She had a shell around her and it was something that I was trying to poke at with a little bit of humour. The reaction was not quite what was intended. The first few times I met her I really think that she thought that I was a bad man. I think she turned the tables on me by simply having better manners than I did right away.

They came back over the next four or five months to work on other songs and Eva started to loosen up. A couple of times when she was in the vocal booth I hooked a device called a harmoniser on her voice; this takes your voice and makes it very low and gruff or very high, like a baby. She didn't know it was coming so she put the headphones on and started talking. It came out very low and gruff. All of a sudden it was like something switched in her and she was doing this impression. She sounded like a big old black dude. She started cussing, just magnificent cadences. She was saying some nasty stuff and I'm thinking, 'Alright! We're seeing a side of her that I like!' I think she started tolerating me and it lightened up the situation a lot, so we worked on the record and she sang and then I didn't see her because the record was finished.

Eva dressed as an Easter bunny at a holiday celebration for underprivileged children organised by her friend Ruth Murphy. Eva agreed to help her friend out on the condition that she wear full costume and make-up to avoid embarrassment. Eva spent the day handing out Easter eggs from a basket and hugging the children.

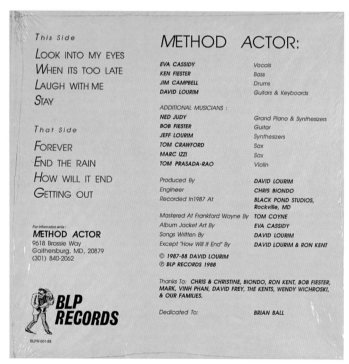

Front and back of Eva's first album cover.

Although music had become Eva's artistic priority, Method Actor was still a long way from the material she wanted to be working on…

Ned Judy I played keyboards and arranged some horns and Eva did the album cover and sang lead and background vocals. She wasn't really into it; it was more rock. It was more from her past when she was into Heart and I wasn't really into it either. But Dave Lourim, the first Stonehenge guitar player, was. So we were doing it to help him out with his project.

Hugh Cassidy She didn't like it; it was pop. She said that to me several times. Her thrust was not really towards doing that kind of music. It was just too banal for her. She was more sophisticated than that. She had a range in all these other directions and knew about what you could really do with a lyric. It was a chance to hear your own voice and take some stock and measure of how you do things, but she did not like it.

Dan Cassidy She sent me a cassette copy of the Method Actor album, which was her first professional recording session pressed on vinyl and released. But she was only asked to sing the songs and had no real control of production. It was very commercially-oriented rock, very saleable stuff. It was pretty much the most 'professional thing' I'd ever heard her do.

In the autumn of 1988, after four years playing violin professionally in Europe, Dan returned home and was struck by the changes that had taken place in Eva…

Dan Cassidy She had actually started to come back to life a little bit. She had quite a nice little social group; she was going out dancing. She was coming out of her shell and there was a direction there. We hung out a lot. I had completely changed, too, and I lifted her up a lot. I was full of beans.

I saw a Method Actor concert at The Bayou rock club in Washington. Eva was very nervous. She hadn't done a concert in years and she was running up and down stairs to alleviate this nervous tension, but she sang incredibly. I came back and said to her, 'How come you're not famous yet?' and she said, 'Oh, I didn't sing very well.'

"She represents all that is good and kind in the world."

Eva's drawing of Chris Biondo's dog presented as payment for studio time.

The sessions for the Method Actor album had been over for some time and Eva's contact with Chris Biondo had come to an end. It was Eva who took the initiative to link up with him again…

Chris Biondo Eva called me one day and said she wanted to get away from her job. She wanted to get out of there and do something else. She said she didn't have a whole lot of money, but she wanted to make a demo tape so she could get jobs singing for people. She wanted to sing some background vocals and I was doing real good at the time, so I was in a position to help her out. I had this really old dog, a beagle, called Bernice. One of the times when Eva was over at my studio when we'd been doing Method Actor, we were standing outside the bottom of the driveway and my dog started scooting down the gravel to scratch her ass on the ground. Eva laughed; she thought that was really funny. I said, 'You shouldn't laugh at her because Bernice represents all that's good and kind in the world.' So when she told me she didn't have much money, I said, 'If you draw me a picture of Bernice, I'll try to help you.' So she said, 'OK.' She came over and the first thing we did was *God Bless the Child* and that ended up on *The Other Side*.

Playing on the session that day was a classically trained pianist named Lenny Williams who would work with Eva many times…

Lenny Williams Chris said, 'This is the best singer I've ever heard,' and I thought, 'Oh yeah, I've heard that before. Guy likes a girl; she sings; all of a sudden she's the best singer in the world.' He was using her to sing back-ups and trying to find her any work he could, because she was working in a nursery and he just thought this girl is too good to be mixing fertiliser.

So she sang the track to *God Bless the Child* or *You've Changed* and I was like – 'Oh, she **is** the best singer I ever heard.' Well, she was definitely at that point the best singer I had ever worked with.

Chris Biondo I'm looking at her and I'm saying, 'What have I got? I've got this secret weapon that I'm working with. She could sing with anyone and she's hanging out with me.' My background music was pop music, I had no jazz background, no folk background and she brought all that stuff out and showed me how good it could be.

Eva remained at Behnke's but, with Chris's help, was able to get extra work singing on sessions across the full range of Washington DC music…

Chris Biondo She did a lot of choruses on rap songs, which would have verses where the guys would talk about how ruthless they are, and then she would sing these beautiful choruses, and then they'd go back talking their stuff again. A lot of the stuff she did was the Oakland sound, where the Tupac thing came from. There were spin-off groups from all that stuff and Eva sang well, so the tracks sounded better.

She had a very neutralising effect. I worked with some guys who had criminal records, who had histories of violence, histories of drug-dealing, just all round not nice guys. She'd come in and they'd stop cursing; they'd apologise if they did by mistake. They loved her.

Chris Biondo began to spend more and more time working on Eva's demos. As tapes were recorded, Eva would take them home for her family to hear…

Barbara Cassidy She didn't talk much about it. But when she started recording and when she

Eva, Missie and Margret.

had a song on tape, she would play it for me. She would ask, 'What did you think Mom? How'd you like that Mom?'

Hugh Cassidy Once in a while she'd say, 'Here's one that we've just finished recording. Would you like to hear it?' and I'd say, 'Sure, put it on.' I think she was interested in having my approval of it, but she turned out to be far more finely nuanced about music and what she wanted to do with it than I was. Her judgment was very accurate and I see that in hindsight.

Every once in a while I'd ask her, 'Do you wanna play?' She'd say, 'OK,' and we'd sit down and she'd get her guitar and we'd play. I'd play the bass and she'd play the guitar and then we'd sing. I'd say, 'You've got too many chords in that song; I don't think it's gonna fly. Who's going to play with you?' So she says, 'Well I'll play it my way by myself then,' and I'd say, 'Well that's what you're going to have to do, because I can't even follow you on it. I don't know what chord you're going to put in next!' I don't think she liked that. We contested over that, but I could probably say in hindsight that her version would have stood the test and flown.

As they worked together Eva and Chris's relationship grew closer, despite their different approaches to life…

'Being nice, liking nature, loving her mother — these were all things that were just ingrained in her and it sounds almost contrived, but when people talk about Eva and say these things, they're not kidding.'

Chris Biondo

Chris Biondo She was a very good sort of person; she seemed to be so considerate of life in a way that others weren't. Once I had a little family of ants trying to get under the door of my kitchen and I was discussing methods of extermination with her and she said, 'Why don't you get a paper plate and put something tasty on it, let them walk on it, catch them and put them out in the woods?' That's not something I would have done. I would have smashed the little bastards and watched them die horribly as they wriggled their legs!

She was spending more time with me, working on her stuff, and we started to do things together. We started to go to movies and spend a lot of time doing things of that nature. We'd eat dinner, get a video, that kind of thing; that was a big change for us. We were friends and I was very respectful of her shyness and being introverted.

The best way I can describe it is: when people are young, they tend to have a certain amount of innocence about them – what you think about people and how you react to them is totally honest, you don't hurt them. She never lost that. The things that go along with being an adult – the relationships, saying bad things about people, the types of things that you can't go through life without doing, were the kind of things that didn't come naturally to her. Being nice, liking nature, loving her mother – these were all things that were just ingrained in her and it sounds almost contrived, but when people talk about Eva and say these things, they're not kidding. To me, if I sang like that, I'd be real stuck-up; but she didn't think that way.

With the exception of the Method Actor concerts, opportunities to perform were rare. However, Eva did sing when first her sister Anette, and then her best friend Ruth Murphy, were married…

Dan Cassidy Dad, Eva and I played at Anette's wedding in 1989, shortly after the Method Actor concert. I rehearsed the two of them and we got a set list together. We played beautifully; we played acoustically in a lovely little room up on a mountain where the wedding was held. Eva looked great; she had flowers in her hair, felt good about herself, sang beautifully and everyone shut up and listened. It was great.

Hugh Cassidy I suspect that she probably did *Over the Rainbow* and a few numbers of that sort. She sang one that we always did, which we sang the harmonies to: *Cotton Fields*. We used to have fun singing harmony with that: '*Oh, when those cotton balls get rotten, you can't get very much cotton, in those old cotton fields back home.*' We had a lot of fun with that. We'd kind of hokey it up and put on accents when we were alone, mess around, and it was a fun little tune.

Barbara Cassidy We had a wonderful crowd. My mother had come in from Germany, and Anette had invited all her family and friends and her husband's family as well. I remember that the crowd woke up when Eva sang *Your Cheating Heart*, the country music song. They thought it was so inappropriate! That was a great day!

Ruth Murphy Eva sang for my wedding. I had to really coax her to try to get her out to sing. She was very shy about getting in front of people and singing, but she went ahead and did it. She sang *Bridge over Troubled Water*. Everyone thought: 'What an unusual song for a wedding,' but I really like the song and I think Eva liked it, too. Everybody was crying and would go up to her and say, 'Eva, what a great job.' She would always graciously say, 'Thank you,' but she was very uncomfortable with all those compliments.

In 1990 Eva sang *Over the Rainbow* to Chris for the first time…

Performing at her sister Anette's wedding, 1989.

Chris Biondo When I first heard *Over the Rainbow* we were doing a bit of a road trip to Ikea furniture, north of Baltimore, and she started singing it in the car. I was in a fairly vulnerable mood, so when I heard it I started crying feebly and I had to pull over and regain my composure to continue the journey safely.

The only thing that was different between *Over the Rainbow,* the way she sang it in the car and the way she recorded it, was she changed two notes. The first note of the song, which was lower, she made higher and she changed the note on the 'far' of 'the clouds are far behind us' – but pretty much her singing *Over the Rainbow* to me in the car is the way you hear it today.

When I first heard Over the Rainbow we were doing a bit of a road trip to Ikea furniture, north of Baltimore, and she started singing it in the car. I was in a fairly vulnerable mood, so when I heard it I started crying feebly and I had to pull over and regain my composure to continue the journey safely.' Chris Biondo

Chris worked with Eva to further her career by suggesting a manager and persuading her the time was right to create her own back-up band…

Chris Biondo I was working with a group called Radiant, which was signed to Columbia Records at the time, and I became friends with them. Their manager was Al Dale. I liked Al because he seemed to be a docile, chipper guy. If you met him and you talked to him, you'd always discover a smile on his face. He's a pleasant fellow and I thought because Eva was a very shy person, that maybe he might be a good fit for her. It wouldn't feel right if Eva was working with someone who was a hardened music guy.

Eva began using Biondo, Lenny Williams, drummer Raice McLeod and Keith Grimes, a local guitarist with a background in R 'n' B, as her regular musicians…

Keith Grimes Chris was really terse, like a guy playing a cop on TV. He said, 'Man, I'm working with a singer; she's great; come on over and listen to this tape.' It's kind of a dicey situation because often you come out and rehearse and listen to the person and it's a matter of, 'How do I diplomatically extricate myself?' So that was what I was braced for really. But then he played me some tapes that they had made together and I realised that she was a great singer.
I didn't know what to expect, but when I did meet Eva, whatever I expected, she wasn't it. When I first saw her, I think I walked into the control room of the studio and looked through the glass and there she was, holding a Fender Stratocaster. Although she was petite and blonde, she looked like a pioneer woman. She looked very hardy; she probably had just come from work over at the tree nursery and she looked like she'd just stepped off the Appalachian Trail. There was something very stalwart-looking about her. She wasn't very ethereal at all; she was right there.

When I met her, I realised she was just as into Aretha Franklin and Ray Charles as I was and so that was really all I needed to know. Eva had a great deal of appreciation for Ray Charles and, in fact, we did four or five Ray Charles songs, or songs that were associated with him: *You Don't Know Me, Drown in My Own Tears*. We really dug brother Ray.

Chris Biondo When we first discussed putting her band together she didn't want to continue to play guitar as well. Keith had to twist her arm to do it. She learned she felt uncomfortable when she wasn't singing and didn't know what to do with her hands, so she gave in.

She was real self-conscious about *Over the Rainbow* because the guitar part was real hard for her and, usually in the middle section where she does the instrumental break, she'd fluff a note or something. If she couldn't play it perfectly, it caused her to feel upset and it kept her from doing it live for a long time. That's a hard song to play on guitar the way she did it.

Chris Biondo She had a few songs that she wanted to do. There was an Aretha Franklin song called *When the Whistle Blows*, and *Angel* by Jimmy Hendrix, and *Bridge Over Troubled Water*. But the problem was, we just didn't have enough songs to play live, so Keith brought over a pile of stuff and taught us to play a couple of dozen songs and that was the thing that gave us enough material.

Keith Grimes Really the whole story of our live performance stuff had to do with the battle of the ballad, because if left to her own devices, she would have done an entire set of ballads. In my estimation, for the kind of places we were playing, two ballads a set is plenty. Eva would bring in songs and they'd all be ballads. Finally I said, 'We need new songs and they can't be ballads,' and the next time, she said, 'I have a song I really want to do,' I said, 'Is it a ballad?' and she said, 'Yeah,' so I said, 'No,' and she was unhappy that I vetoed her ballad. I think she felt like she could really get down deep in her soul in those tunes, in a way that she couldn't on some of the other things.

Chris Biondo There were some up-tempo things that she picked and liked to do, like *Route 66*, but there were some songs she wasn't too crazy about, like *Respect*. That was the most popular song we did and I thought it was kind of important that we do it, because you save your big guns for the end. If you want to go out smoking, you've just got to play *Respect*. Everyone loved it; she liked the song. She just didn't think she sang it good enough. The only complaint that I ever got from her about the stuff was the song *Respect* and that was because I kept pushing it. That was a sore spot between us.

Lenny Williams Eva hated singing that, hated it, because it was so identified with Aretha. But she wailed on it; she'd bring the house down on it. She'd just be Aretha when she did it. But she just hated doing it, because I think she just thought it was a little too overdone. I think her heart was in the ballad stuff, but if you saw her live you'd say, 'Oh, she's just a knock-you-to-the-back-of-the-wall blues singer.' Because she could do that stuff; she could blow anybody off the stage with that stuff.

Keith Grimes There are some people that get into performing because they really want to have attention paid to them and they say, 'All right, I'm going to work up a skill that will justify my getting up on stage.' And then there are other people who are strictly into music and don't care about that, and Eva would definitely be in the latter category. She did want to be appreciated, but she didn't want to get out there and just have everybody fall in love with her. She wasn't a dynamic on-stage performer. She rarely said anything between songs. Sometimes we'd say, 'Eva, OK, next set we want you to just say one thing,' and she would, and it would be three words.

The intensity of Eva's performances and her demeanour on stage meant that the act sometimes failed to translate or left the audience uncomfortable. The problem was especially acute on the nightclub circuit…

Chris Biondo We emptied rooms. We played at places where people would be sitting in front of us while Eva did *Over the Rainbow*, cackling while they ate their dinner, and it drove me nuts. It just absolutely baffled me, but *Over the Rainbow* just didn't translate. There were a couple of times when I had to go up to people and just say, 'I hope that you leave soon.' Eva got real mad at me. We were playing at a club and I stopped the band and I looked at this lady sitting a couple of tables over and I said, 'Excuse me. Are we playing too loud, can you hear yourself talk?' Eva never sang a bad job in her life, even when she had a bad job.

'When I met her I realised she was just as into Aretha Franklin and Ray Charles as I was and so that was really all I needed to know. Eva had a great deal of appreciation for Ray Charles and, in fact, we did four or five Ray Charles songs, or songs that were associated with him: You Don't Know Me, Drown in My Own Tears. We really dug brother Ray'

Keith Grimes

Chris Biondo She liked it when there weren't that many people in the audience.
She'd say, 'How many people are out there?' and I'd say, 'It's not looking good, Eva,
I counted 17,' and she'd say, 'Oh, that's good.'
If there were a lot of people in the house, then there were more people to be disapproving
of her. If she had a room that was not happening that much and people didn't care,
then in a strange kind of warped way, she preferred that. I think it was just the fact that
she felt even her playing guitar in front of anybody was maybe a waste of their time,
she didn't think it was worthy. I don't think there was a person that hung around with
Eva that hadn't told her she was the best singer they ever heard. I never heard anybody
sing as good as Eva.

'I don't think there was a person

that hung around with Eva that hadn't

told her she was the best singer

they ever heard.'

Chris Biondo

Meanwhile Dan was trying to make a connection that he hoped would help Eva make a breakthrough…

Dan Cassidy I knew a girl from Bowie who was dating Daniel Lanois, who was a famous producer. They were living in New Orleans. I was invited to meet them and I had a very good demo tape of Eva's with me, stuff she had been doing with Chris Biondo – very nice recordings of R 'n' B, the collection of tunes that we hear now. My flight got bumped off in Chicago and I never got to New Orleans and you never know what would have happened. That could have easily turned into something. But I remained really optimistic for Eva.

Performing with friends (from left) Chris Izzi, Eva, Larry Melton and Joe Knaggs.

'She did some songs on guitar with Chuck, and she did Over the Rainbow. It was a real crowd-pleaser, a show-stopper.'

Chris Biondo

Let the Good Times Roll

Chuck Brown I was on my way back, walking up the hill to my limousine, and I seen this cute, little-short, beautiful, little blonde lady with little shorts on, and she looked less than five feet tall and she had such a beautiful pleasant look on her face. Then she started smiling as she got closer to me and she said, 'Hi, I'm Eva Cassidy; you're Chuck Brown,' and I thought, 'My God!' All Chris had told me was her name. I hadn't asked him how old she was, whether she was white or black or whatever. Oh man, it was the shock of my life!

In Washington DC Chuck Brown is a legend. He is the 'Godfather of Go-Go': the city's home-grown dance music that fills dancehalls in Washington's black neighbourhoods. Go-go is a high-energy, rhythmic funk combined with call-and-response audience participation. It is a sound that Chuck Brown, son of a share-cropper from North Carolina, and ex-con gone straight, created single-handedly...

Chuck Brown Go-go is very energetic and communicating with the audience is one of the main things. The better you can do that, the longer you'll last and the more you'll be appreciated. We'd start off on a top 40 song, do about half that song, cut it short, break it down into the percussion and talk to the audience. That's when they started getting up on those tables and taking off those neckties. If you want to pack a house, you do go-go.

Go-go depends on the relationship between the performer and the audience. In 1990, when Chuck Brown arrived at Chris Biondo's studio to work on his go-go version of the Willie Dixon classic, *Hoochie Coochie Man*, the audience had become the problem. DC was ravaged by crack-cocaine-related violence in the 1980s and early 1990s and some of the shootings associated with the problem took place in and around the go-go club scene. Chuck, the originator of go-go, was disgusted…

Chuck Brown I wanted to get away from go-go for a while. I was sick of it. There wasn't no violence at my shows, but I feared that stuff transferring, I didn't want to play. 'Chuck why don't you play?' 'Because you all don't know how to act.' They were acting like a bunch of damn fools; it was getting ugly, crazy people and thugs, coming to my shows holding big ass signs up in my face all night, with those big thug names on them. I got sick of that; I got grouchy; I'm an old man, it don't take much to make me grouchy. So I wanted to get away from that. I didn't want to hear no go-go music, I stopped listening to the radio.

The question for Chuck was where else he could go musically. He found the answer at Chris Biondo's studio…

Chris Biondo I was doing lots of go-go records and Chuck Brown is the guy who created it. He's the guy who, if you're doing that kind of music, you want to have come to your studio, and finally, after I had for years recorded other people, he came to my studio. I was terrified of the guy. He's wearing a big leather jacket with the fringe, got a cigar in his mouth, sunglasses, and a cowboy hat with a dead snake on the front, yet he comes in and he's really, really polite.
I liked him. I thought, 'I wanna hang with this guy because he's just so nice to me.' So we were working on the song and he went upstairs to the bathroom and he found a bottle of vodka that a friend of mine had brought back from the Soviet Union. He brought it down and said, 'What we gonna do with this?' I don't

drink but I said, 'Let's drink it.' So I kind of broke my no-drinking law and we started on this bottle of vodka, mixed it with vermouth and started getting loose. We were hangin' – we were guys and I was sitting with Chuck Brown.

As the vodka martinis took effect, Chris decided to put into practise a plan he had conceived, but considered a long shot…

Chris Biondo It must have been two or three in the morning. I had a two-hour tape of everything I'd done with Eva on it and I just started playing it and he listened to the whole thing. He just hung in there. He was a trooper and we sat there and I played him the whole thing and then I rewound the tape to the beginning and let it run again. Chuck had mentioned that he liked jazz and he wanted to do jazz and Eva had done *God Bless the Child*. I was thinking that if Chuck liked the way she sang, they might be able to record something together and that might help Eva a lot. I thought there probably wasn't much of a chance, because Chuck is a very big icon around here, but he seemed to be primed and I hit him with it.

Chuck Brown He put this cassette on and this sweet, mellow, rich voice came out singing *Call it Stormy Monday*. My God, why did she have to sing that one? That was my favourite song and when I heard the first two or three notes of that song I had goose bumps. It really took me out, and I said, 'Who's that?' and he told me, 'It's a young lady by the name of Eva.'

Celebrating their first recording session: (from left) Chuck Brown's wife Jocelyn Brown, Chuck Brown, Lenny Williams, drummer Ju-Ju House, Chris Biondo.

Chris Biondo He listened and we sat there and we talked and we drank. I pretty much had the songs to the point where I knew where all the good notes were, so, if he was talking and I knew something was coming up, I'd shut him up, I'd try to pinpoint the real good points for him. I told him this was a girl that was recording here and that I thought she was the greatest singer in the world. Every time I'd play something he was like: 'Yeah, yeah, I love that.' He was being very, very enthusiastic and he didn't look like he was blowing his brains out to get the hell out of there. When he left the next day the sun was coming up.

Chuck Brown I guess there were about four songs on there that I grew up with and I'm thinking – her voice is really sweet and young, but her style and the way that she sings these songs, I'm thinking she's a mature maybe thirty-eight to forty year old. I said to

Chris, 'I would love to do a song with her,' and he said, 'You can,' and he gave me a copy of the tape. I was driving my limousine that night. I put that tape in, and my back speakers are big ones back there, and I played that tape all the way home.

Chris Biondo I talked to Chuck the next day and I said, 'Bring your limousine.' Then I told Eva and she just smiled – she couldn't believe it. She said, 'I'm going to meet him?' I said, 'Yeah, you're going to sing with him, so you get to meet him – that's how it works.'

Ruth Murphy Oh, she couldn't wait. I remember before she even started. She was so excited and she was excited that I knew who Chuck Brown was. Because in my surroundings Chuck Brown was really huge, in my high school. I mean he's the godfather of go-go. It was, 'Oh my God, Chuck Brown!' So that was very exciting for her. She felt it was a huge honour to be able to sing with him.

For Eva, the opportunity was obvious; and for Chuck, the proposed collaboration was a dream come true, and a chance to reduce his involvement in the troubled go-go scene...

Chuck Brown I'd never done jazz before I met Eva Cassidy, so she was the turning point in my career. Jazz to me, and blues to me, were only in my head, my memory, my mind and my wishes. When I heard her sing, she gave me the nerve. I wouldn't go out there by myself. I wanted to go out there like Louis Armstrong and Ella Fitzgerald, and when I heard her voice my mind was made up. Just the fact that she knew about these things – stuff that was here before she was born, that I grew up with – was amazing to me. When we met, we went back into the studio and Chris said, 'Now you guys want to do a record?' and I said, 'I sure do.' So the first track we cut was *You've Changed*.

By the time Chris Biondo played Chuck the tape, he and Eva were growing closer still. Chris, who had recently come through a divorce, wondered whether there was a prospect of a romantic relationship...

Chris Biondo We spent a lot of time together and I had suggested to her that maybe we oughta try being in a relationship. She didn't think that was a good idea and I thought I'd really kind of crossed a line with her. But she called me up the next day and it was fine and we didn't talk about it for a couple of weeks.

Ruth Murphy Chris was just coming out of his divorce at right about the same time they met and I remember Eva talking about it: 'I really like this guy, there's something different about him.'

Chris Biondo It was the summer of 1990, after the first session with Chuck, and we were at King's Dominion theme park. We were sitting outside and she said, 'Wanna go to the Virgin Islands next month?' I said, 'Alright,' and we got tickets and from that point on, I guess I figured things had changed.

With Chris Biondo outside his studio in Glendale, Maryland.

10615

The sessions for Eva and Chuck's album *The Other Side* were organised around Chris's studio schedule and Eva's work commitments and came together over an extended period between 1990 and 1991. For Eva, *The Other Side* was a project she could tackle with enthusiasm, particularly as it drew on the 1930s and 1940s influences she loved as a child. It is an album largely made up of jazz and blues standards including *Let the Good Times Roll, Fever* and *God Bless the Child*, but it also includes a version of Chips Moman's and Dan Penn's sixties soul-classic, *Dark End of the Street* and Eva's solo recording of *Over the Rainbow…*

Chris Biondo   My favourite is *You Don't Know Me*. We worked on that in a way that I think people who do duets ought to do. It was night, we had the lights off; I had the singers sit in two different booths facing each other, so when they're trading off parts, one encourages the other and gives ideas. I just listened to them. We worked on it for four or five hours. It was just beautiful, it was a good time.

Chuck Brown   Her voice was like honey and cream. When you heard her sing, there's not a flaw. I never heard her make a mistake. Of course she'd say, 'Oh Chuck, we got to do that again; I made a mistake there,' but it sounded so good to me. The cut that really stands out for me is the first one we did – *You've Changed, the Sparkle in Your Eye is Gone*. The way she hit that. There is no doubt about it that is my favourite that we did together. And I like the one that she sings by herself, *God Bless the Child*, and I like *Dark End of the Street*.

The collaboration with Chuck Brown was an amazing leap into the local big league for Eva, especially as the duo were booked for concert appearances at prestigious venues like the Blues Alley jazz club in Georgetown…

Chris Biondo   Eva sang; Chuck talked. Sometimes Chuck would forget his lines and Eva would sing them for him and save his ass. Sometimes they'd be so spot on, it would be great. It was just a really fun time. He took the heat off her, loosened her up and once in a while she'd say, 'Thank you.' It worked. She did some songs on guitar with Chuck, and she did *Over the Rainbow*. It was a real crowd-pleaser, a show-stopper.

'Her voice was like honey and cream. When you heard her sing, there's not a flaw. I never heard her make a mistake.'

Chuck Brown

FAR LEFT Eva and Chuck Brown cover photo from *The Other Side*.

Keith Grimes Chuck was great; he had clout. He was established, so we got some good jobs. Although, privately, Chuck has almost as much stage nerves as Eva, you'd never know it because he gets out there and he has no problems talking to an audience and just behaving in a way that puts everybody at ease and is charming. He would play off of Eva, look at her, move in her direction and she was able to respond and work off of him and be a little more extroverted than she would have been otherwise, because it's hard to be uptight when somebody's just kind of goofing around.

Chuck Brown She didn't talk that much and I'm a mouthy old guy, but there was great chemistry there. The band knew everything we were going to do; the band was real tight. We went to Blues Alley and we both were nervous, both about the same. I'm walking back and forth and she walked by again and I say something funny to make her laugh and she's walking this way and I'm walking that way and she says, 'Chuck, I'm scared,' and I say, 'Me too, we're supposed to be scared Eva. That's what makes it right, but once you get out there, once you hit those first two or three notes, it's all over.'

Hugh Cassidy When Chuck got up on stage, she could look at him and smile and pretend that she knew what she was doing and snap her fingers. The number of singers are two now, not one, and so the 'enemy' (the audience) is divided. 'They all can't look at me; half of them have to look at Chuck, and then when I'm not singing, I can look at Chuck instead of having to engage with the audience,' and so it helped her in that sense.

Washington newspaper advertisement for Eva and Chuck Brown at Blues Alley.

Lenny Williams Chuck, in his element doing go-go, is the ultimate. He really is in touch with the crowd. But doing the smaller jazz gigs, the smaller clubs where it's more intimate and there's less to hide behind, he was still Chuck and he was still good, but he was less comfortable. So Chuck wasn't the master of that in those situations. He was more nervous about the music; she was more nervous about being on stage – so together they evened each other out. Musically she was right there for him and if he dropped a line or forgot where he was, she'd jump in. I mean she was the seasoned performer in that respect, as far as knowing her material. In between songs Chuck would go into his patter, which was usually pretty good.

Chris Biondo There were a couple of scary moments. We played at Wolf Trap, opening for the Neville Brothers and it was sold out. That was scary. It was maybe ten times as many people as she'd ever played for in one place before. You walk out on stage and it's a football stadium full of people. Eva was just like, 'Oooh!' It gives you a terrible feeling; your stomach's tied in knots; you're a little shaky; your heart's beating fast; you might have a real concern about remembering what you have to do. That was the big step. She was nervous and shaking a little bit, walking out in front of these people. Had to be really strong, emotional, scary stuff for her, but she kicked ass. She just went out and sang.

Barbara Cassidy It was nice to see Eva on the stage with the spotlight on her. She reminded me a little bit of Marlene Dietrich. She was dressed beautifully in high heels and it was just a magnificent evening. When I saw her like that, I thought: 'That's my Eva!' and the sense of maternal pride I had in her was great.

With Chuck Brown at Wolf Trap, 1994.

Margret Cassidy As the crowds got bigger and she got recognition, she was real pleased with that. It was like an added bonus, but it never got to her head. The word that always comes to mind is 'overwhelmed' and even on tape you'll hear her say, 'I'm so overwhelmed.' That's how she was with all the attention and all the praise. She was overwhelmed – pleasantly.

When Chris opted to relocate his home and studio from Rockville, he asked Eva to move in with him. The move represented a significant step for Eva, who had only previously lived away from the family home for one brief period…

Barbara Cassidy She didn't do it on an impulse. She said, 'Shall I do it Mom; should I not?' And then Eva decided. 'Yes, I'll give it a try with Chris,' and that was OK with me as long as they were happy together. He was so kind. He bent over backwards to please her and I thought it was the most wonderful thing that somebody would get spoiled so much and catered to and pampered. That was great. And Chris recognised her wonderful voice and really encouraged her to record as much as possible, so we are enormously grateful for what he did for Eva.

Ruth Murphy It was kind of a neat adult relationship for Eva as far as I was concerned. Chris really did wonderful things for her. He was an amazingly important person in Eva's life, probably the single most influential person.

He really paid attention to who she was and all the different facets of her. He attempted to really understand Eva. He listened to her and sometimes volunteered his time to record her music.

Celia Murphy They really did care for each other and I think they were both just really comfortable and very willing to show each other off. Chris would always say stuff like, 'Isn't she great?' or, 'Isn't she something?' and Eva would just kind of roll her eyes shyly and go, 'Oh.' And then she would say something about Chris, and I think that was good for Eva.

Chris Biondo We went swimming a lot, we rode our bikes, we used to walk the dog, we liked renting movies. She wasn't big on gourmet things. She loved pizzas and she loved tuna-fish sandwiches and we were known to buy hot dogs from 7-11 on a regular basis.

Her favourite movie was *The Color Purple*. She loved the music. She loved the whole character Whoopi Goldberg played. She also liked *Empire of the Sun* and *Pulp Fiction*, though I remember she didn't like *Ghost*. We did not like that movie at all; we walked out of it before the end – thought it was pretty hokey.

From time to time she would put on a dress and get dressed up, but it was something she couldn't wait to get out of. She mostly wore my clothes. She'd find a shirt or something that she liked and she'd wear that, jeans and work boots.

LEFT With Chris Biondo.

RIGHT On holiday in the Virgin Islands, 1993.

We went to the Virgin Islands four or five times and spent a lot of time snorkelling. At a place called Barnacle Bill's they had an open mike and it was packed. The list was fifty people long and the one thing that they always did when somebody finished singing was to say, 'OK, that was great, goodbye.' Well, she went up there and did *Drown in My Own Tears* and they asked her to play another song and then another.

In 1992 Eva's brother, Dan, returned to Europe, this time permanently, to pursue his musical career…

Dan Cassidy Around that time I left to go to Iceland. I was unhappy by this time, my 'full of beans' had run out. I got caught in the rat race, got the wrong day job. Eva saw I was unhappy and I was getting down, and getting bored and uninspired and complaining. She just said, 'Dan, if you want to leave, go – go off. If travelling is what you want to do, do it. If you get your energy back through travelling, go.' So I just dropped a good day job, a new car and an excellent band job for a no-guarantee and uncertainty in Iceland.

The attention and acclaim that followed *The Other Side* had started to attract serious record company interest. Blue Note is one of America's most illustrious jazz labels. Its president is Bruce Lundvall…

Bruce Lundvall I got a call from an independent A & R guy called Andy Fuhrman. He said, 'I have a girl here who's just wonderful,' so I said, 'Great, bring her up,' and he came to my office in New York with Eva. There was this really wonderful-looking woman, with long blonde hair and big blue eyes, with a very spiritual, beatific look on her face and with a very quiet voice when she spoke.
She had nothing to play to me – nothing on tape or anything. She didn't even have a guitar on her. So she just stood in the middle of my office and sang *Amazing Grace* a cappella and I just absolutely fell apart. I said, 'Oh my God, what an amazing voice!'

'I knew Eva really quite well.

I met her when I was starting a jazz club

in Washington DC.

I wanted to find out who the local talent

was and have them play at the club.

She played regularly at the club.

I played with her many times.

Mick Fleetwood

It was incredibly powerful, but the thing that really killed me was when she sang softly. It was so, so beautiful.

I never heard anything like that in my life. It was incredible. Her voice would just freeze me. I thought she was absolutely wonderful. So we talked about direction and she said she just liked to sing songs that she loved and that covered a wide span of material. So I listened to some of the stuff she had done with Chuck Brown and some other stuff. But it was all over the place, so I didn't know what to do.

Chris Biondo Blue Note said, 'Go record some songs. We don't have any idea of what to do with you. Record some songs and send it to us and then we can figure out what we can do with you.' So she decided what to record. She did *Golden Thread, Songbird, Blues in the Night* and *Nightbird*. So you got the gospel song, you got the traditional jazz song, you got the country slow tune and you got the pop. And it was really something they were baffled by 'What direction is this? This is four songs and I don't get it.'

Eva had also come to the attention of Fleetwood Mac drummer Mick Fleetwood, whose club, Fleetwood's, had opened in Washington…

Mick Fleetwood I knew Eva really quite well. I met her when I was starting a jazz club in Washington DC. I wanted to find out who the local talent was and have them play at the club. She played regularly at the club. I played with her many times.

Bruce Lundvall had not given up on Eva, but was searching for a way to harness her talents…

Bruce Lundvall It kind of drifted for a bit – I still thought she was brilliant. I just didn't know what to with her. So then I put her together with a band called Pieces Of A Dream. They were a three-piece from Philadelphia, and they knew about Eva. They'd heard about her and they said, 'OK, let's use her.' They were a kind of jazz, R 'n' B outfit and I had a nice, commercial song called *Goodbye Manhattan* and Eva ended up singing it, and they made an album together. It appeared on that. It was a nice ballad, with a big, big chorus and a funky feeling to it, and she nailed it. She went on tour with them for a while. She did just two songs. We actually released *Goodbye Manhattan* as a single, but it didn't do much.

Chris Biondo There were two songs, *Have a Little Faith*, which she thought sounded like she was singing in a beauty pageant contest, and *Goodbye Manhattan*, about a special bond or some kind of special relationship that somebody has with Manhattan; but there are not enough woods in New York City for Eva to feel that good about it. Anyway, she finally got a record; they sent it to her and I think she left it in her trunk.

Barbara Cassidy I don't know if it was a mutual thing or on whose decision, but she wasn't thrilled, to be honest. There is a little picture inside the record jacket when they put make-up on her and she said, 'Mom, I was in tears because of what they were doing to my face.' She didn't want other people to dominate her. I kind of admired her for her spunk because, if she hadn't been happy, it would have been miserable touring and doing something you really don't enjoy doing.

It is unclear how Eva came to leave Pieces Of A Dream; but it seems certain that while she did her best to fit in with that group, and with Blue Note generally, her artistic principles and own sense of what she wanted outweighed any commercial considerations…

'If she had money, it was great and if she didn't, she didn't need it. People were complaining about the price of gasoline going up a few years ago and she said, "I don't know what they're talking about. I still get five dollars' worth."'

Barbara Cassidy

Chris Biondo Over the years at least half-a-dozen, maybe more, people from major labels – I'm not talking about little indies – the big guys – came down and saw her. When one of the labels came down, Eva came to the studio and we put in a tape and she went into the vocal room and sang to the tape for this guy. He had this record-company, kind of jive thing going on, saying, 'What do you want to do, what direction do you want to go in?' Her answer was, 'Anything but that pop crap.' The guy's got his guys with him, to check out this talent in Washington, and she's said the magic words to make him go away for ever. And he went away and we never saw him again.

Lenny Williams She just didn't want to sing a lot of pop crap, didn't want to be the next Mariah Carey, didn't want to be Whitney. And what made the record companies most interested in her was that she had the ability to be a Whitney, a Mariah – a diva with a huge range and a powerful voice who could sing in a very R 'n' B style at the drop of a hat. But I don't think that's where her heart was.

Ruth Murphy She would wonder why it just wasn't happening, but at the same time she did acknowledge that she wasn't going to sing a certain kind of song. She wasn't interested in the money and fame and she didn't have the drive. So she was sad that it didn't come to her, but she didn't want to sell herself out for one second. She wasn't going to prance around on stage; she wasn't going to wear fancy clothes.

Barbara Cassidy If she had money, it was great and if she didn't, she didn't need it. People were complaining about the price of gasoline going up a few years ago and she said, 'I don't know what they're talking about. I still get five dollars' worth.' She had a sort of carefree attitude about money; but if she saw something really nice, like a good art book, then she would spend whatever it cost because it was important to her. Making a lot of money was never one of her goals. Being rich and famous never entered her mind – ever.

Anette Cassidy I saw that she had all this talent and I've always been a very goal-driven person and needed to feel successful in some ways to feel good about myself. Eva didn't seem to have that. I just couldn't understand it. She was just happy having fun with her music, just having fun with the art, and she really didn't think in terms of going anywhere with it. I saw the potential and it frustrated me that she wasn't taking advantage of it. I think, in the end, she really ended up teaching me a lot about what's really important in life – that success isn't necessarily the thing that's going to make you happy. You need to enjoy what you're doing and I think she did that.

Driving the tractor
at Behnke's nursery.

In the meantime she carried on working at her job at Behnke's nursery…

Barbara Cassidy She learned how to work the tractor.That was a goal of hers, sitting up on this huge tractor and grinning from ear to ear. She enjoyed that, mowing the fields and then, in the springtime, when the big bags of mulch arrived, the whole gang would have to go and unload the huge tractor-trailers. In those days the girls wanted to have a beautiful tan and she was getting that as a bonus, she thought.

Then, in 1993, she visited her doctor…

Barbara Cassidy She had a little mole on her nose; and it had always bothered her, all her life. She thought it didn't look good, so for vanity reasons she went to a dermatologist and asked for it to be removed. She also pointed out a mole that she had on her back. They did a biopsy on it and it turned out to be malignant. So, she went into surgery.

Chris Biondo I took her to the hospital and got there at seven. I sat out there until eight o'clock, nine, ten, eleven, twelve, one – and then a guy comes out with a photograph of her back and says, 'She's got to stay the night.' I said, 'What, you just took a mole off her back.' He says, 'No, we took all the skin from the base of her neck to the tip of her spine and about four or five inches wide.' He showed me a picture. It looked like they'd just sliced a whole section of her back out.

Barbara Cassidy They removed some more tissue around it. And just to be on the safe side, they removed more than was actually cancerous. They said it hadn't gone deep, that it was very superficial but that we'd have to keep an eye on it and hope for the best.

Hugh Cassidy The doctor assured us that he felt he had got it in time. He dug rather deep, so she was in a little bit of pain and had a bandage on it for a while.

Ruth Murphy When Eva discovered she had melanoma, she downplayed it completely with me. We talked about it at the swimming pool. They took a piece off her back and she had a nasty little scar, but she did not make a big deal out of it. She thought that it was just because of working outside at Behnke's, because she loved the outdoors and it's just natural. I didn't know she was supposed to go back for her check-ups to make sure that the cancer was completely removed off her back. I asked her, 'Eva, you were supposed to go to check-ups?' She was like, 'Oh, something like that.' She was very nonchalant about that.

Chris Biondo I took her once for an MRI where she drank the radioactive stuff and got on the machine and stuff. So I know that at least that one time she was going in to check it out and I thought they got it.

'I just couldn't understand it. She was just happy having fun with her music, just having fun with the art, and she really didn't think in terms of going anywhere with it.'

Anette Cassidy

'She just loved her Mom to bits.

Her Mom was her best friend. They would sit

and just chat for hours about all kinds of things.'

Ruth Murphy

Fields of Gold

Apart from music, the most important facets of Eva Cassidy's life were nature, art and, perhaps most important of all, her relationship with her mother, Barbara…

Barbara Cassidy She was more interested in her peers as a teenager, rather than hanging around her Mom. But that closeness came again when she was in her early twenties and then we were very, very close for the rest of her life. She told everybody that I was her best friend and that's the nicest thing a child can say about you really.

Chris Biondo Her Mom was the most important thing in her life. Barbara is a person who is almost too good for this world. She just doesn't have any mean in her and she doesn't understand mean. She came from a pretty hard childhood and grew up in a very dangerous situation, and she has just been a very calming factor. I love her and I see where Eva got it.

Ruth Murphy She just loved her Mom to bits. Her Mom was her best friend. They would sit and just chat for hours about all kinds of things. Eva loved the German heritage that her Mom came with and she would use words like *Liebchen*. She just loved spending time with her Mom, thought she was one of nature's best gifts to the world. Barbara has always been very gentle. She was very positive for Eva. She seemed very in tune with Eva's feelings, her ups or her downs. She just loved Eva for who Eva was and I think Eva really appreciated that.

Eva's love of nature never diminished. Sundays were reserved for time with her mother – walking, hiking or cycling in the countryside of southern Maryland…

Barbara Cassidy We spent just about every Sunday together. We would drive off to southern Maryland, to some nice rural places, maybe visit some historic mansions or some beautiful gardens, or go bicycle riding, or go to the beach and look for some shells or beach glass. That is just something she so enjoyed and I did too.

We had a lot of common interests. We could talk about how we felt and we were more friends than mother and daughter. We would talk about pretty much anything – world events, things that pleased her, relationships, friendships. And she never wanted anything to go sour with her friendships – that was most important to her. I never pressed her on things. We were both very, very at ease with each other. She was also a very good listener and that's a wonderful thing in a person.

She always had this yearning to be out in the open country and, if possible, by the water. In fall we would take trips into the mountains for the freedom that she felt she needed. And no traffic! It was just lovely and what was so wonderful on these trips was that all her senses were always aware. Nothing escaped her ever. She said, 'Mom, look at this, look at that,' and I would have just passed this by, not taking it in, but she did. She so enriched my life. It was amazing.

Barbara in Novia Scotia.

Bicycle riding was another of her favourite activities. She was always calling people saying, 'Can you go biking with me?' And if one couldn't do it, she'd call the next one to have somebody to come along with her. We did some. She had a bicycle carrier on her car, so we could attach the bicycles and go to a nice spot and take them off and pedal away. She would drive a car into the Old Town of Alexandria and there is a beautiful bicycle path all the way into Washington. She would do that, then browse around the galleries.

She was a very good friend of mine. She was also a travelling companion. We started taking vacations together, going to Nova Scotia. She adored Nova Scotia, where she met some of my family, she just absolutely loved that country up there. She loved it because there was so much peace and quiet. We went in the worst time here in the Washington area, summer. In July and August it gets so humid you just yearn to get away. Up there, there was always a breeze from the ocean and there were very friendly people. She was drawn to the water all her life. That was like a magnet and her biggest dream was to have a little house by the ocean. That was how far her dreams went.

Eva found a deep connection to her cousin Walter Wunderlich, a fine cabinet maker. They shared the same interests and values such as music, nature and protection of the environment. Hansel and Gretel come to mind when I saw them interact. One of the highlights of their lives must have been the evening sitting on the rocks of Cape John, Nova Scotia, watching the sunset, the full moon rise and taking in the spectacular meteor showers. This was a magical experience for both of them. Eva painted a picture of that event and gave it to Walter.

LEFT Eva and Barbara found this abandoned farmhouse when holidaying in Nova Scotia.

Barbara and Eva also took trips to Europe together, visiting Barbara's family in Germany and travelling on to the Greek Islands…

Barbara Cassidy We went first to Germany. It was late May and we went to this area where my sister lives out in the countryside. There were many, many apple trees. They were all in full bloom and Eva was just ecstatic, taking in all this beauty. My sister said that was one of the most beautiful days in May they had ever had. And Eva loved the architecture, the beautiful farmhouse, the thatched roofs, the pastures and the Holstein cows. We continued on with my sister to the island of Samos, which is in the Mediterranean – a Greek island, a volcanic island with very steep mountains. We did a lot of hiking together, the three of us. We stayed on the north side, in the Nightingale Valley, and I remember Eva saying, 'This is heaven.' So later we went back to that very same spot. It had this gorgeous view over the Mediterranean, with the vineyards and the olive trees. We got talking to a farmer who picked some ripe oranges off the tree and gave them to us. He invited us into his little brick house, right in the vineyards, and made us a strong coffee and had some little treats for us. It was wonderful; it was just wonderful! And Eva was just totally enthralled!

Eva had bought a little travel guitar and there, on the island of Samos, in the hotel, we could go up on the roof. My sister said, 'Eva, why don't we all go up there in the evening and you start playing and singing your music?' She did and she enjoyed it – with the beautiful starry sky and the moon rising. After a few days we could tell the rest of the people in the hotel were opening their windows when she sang. One evening we had planned something else and the rest of the people in the hotel said, 'Why didn't you sing tonight?' My sister said to me recently that Eva's voice is still there in the Nightingale Valley. The memories keep coming back. She had so enriched my life, I can't describe it. Those are precious memories, absolutely precious.

In Samos, the Greek Islands.

Eva had a gift for making others see the beauty of nature, as she had on her trips to the woods with Ned Judy in high school. He remained a friend…

Ned Judy Every time I came home, she would probably be the first person I'd see. I'd come home to visit my parents and there she was. She'd come and pick me up and take me out. She was so excited. She wanted to show me some new place she'd discovered. We clicked really well when we were out in the woods. She took me to St Mary's City in Maryland, because she really liked hiking down there. It was peaceful along the river and in the woods.

Hugh Cassidy She certainly was able to see beauty. She'd point it out all the time and she had this great affinity for light. You could see it in her paintings, but also she'd bring it out to you if you didn't see it. If you ever went on any woods walk with her, she'd see how the light was hitting the leaves, or how it's just coming through a little pass, or the shading of the mountainside, or the way sunlight hits the water. Her favourite time was what she

called 'the golden time' – that time when the shadows lengthen and the reddish-gold of the sun as it's going down casts its lengthy rays and then fades into the blue-black. It's a quite magical time, with its shadows and silhouettes, and she would go out at certain times of the day in order to be in the place that she wanted to be at the time when the sun was beginning its descent. She brought a lot to us. She caused us to sense a little more than we would see otherwise, and to appreciate what we were seeing in new ways.

Barbara Cassidy She loved all living things and her senses were always open and aware. If she saw a little bug upside down she, would turn him over and let him run, or if we would go to a fishing pier and people had left invisible fishing lines there, she would get so annoyed. She would roll them up and put them away in a trashcan. And she'd snip the plastic on the six-packs apart, so that no animal would get its head stuck in there and suffocate.
She had this little pick-up truck and once, all of a sudden, she was swerving on this empty country road. I said, 'What are you doing?' and she said, 'Mom, don't you see?' There were woolly bears, little brown caterpillars, all over the road and she didn't want to drive over them.

St Mary's City,
Maryland's first capital.

Elaine Stonebraker shared Eva's interest in both art and the outdoors. She would introduce Eva to a singer named Grace Griffith.

Elaine Stonebraker Our love of the outdoors and our artistic natures gave us a lot in common. What a joy it was to pack a lunch and abandon our cars for a few hours of freedom. We took a week every year as well, to camp and bike on the C & O Canal. Eva loved to travel during what she called 'the golden time', that period at the end of an afternoon when the setting sun casts a glow over everything not in its shadows.
There was one weekend that stands out. I had raved to Eva about the wonderful voice of southern Maryland singer, Grace Griffith. When Grace was scheduled for a concert at Farthing's Ordinary Tavern in historical St Mary's City, of course we had to go. It was one of the best concerts I ever attended. We were thrilled to enjoy it from the first row. The rest of the weekend was spent listening to Grace's earlier material, making polymer beads and listening to Judy Collins albums in my small closet studio. Oh yes – and biking!

But this sensitivity to the natural world had its downside…

Barbara Cassidy She had Seasonal Affective Disorder. When it became September, the days got shorter and she said, 'Mom, I can't really enjoy fall, as beautiful as it is, because I know winter is coming.' In winter she wouldn't have as much energy as she would when the light was bright. But we still went out for outings, because sometimes we'd have these wonderful cold, sunny winter days and she made the best of it. She just didn't have as much energy at that time of year. It was a drab feeling, the winter blues, deprivation of daylight.

We had nice talks and I always checked the newspaper for the sunrise and sunset. Then in December, when the days start getting longer by a minute a day, I would send her a postcard where she was living and she thought that was the greatest thing. 'Oh Mom, I'm so glad you sent me this card. Now I'm looking forward to spring again.' So I always made sure I would let her know when the day with least daylight had passed.

And on her birthday, 2nd February, she always wanted a huge birthday cake with sugar roses on top. She'd take one sugar rose and put it in the freezer. On the first day of spring she took it out and that to her was the biggest holiday, the twenty-first of March. That was her time, that was when she came alive. It was like she was new-born again.

Margret Cassidy Winters are bad. I know specifically so for Eva and me and my Dad. The lack of sunlight and the cold temperatures, and no green and blue out there – everything's grey and brown and dreary and ugly. The sunlight has a lot to do with it. So Eva was definitely a spring girl. She hated winter, and so do I.

Larry Melton She could get very sad sometimes. I think her art really was the sanctuary. I mean, she was never without some sort of big project. I think the art thing was really her little quiet place. She didn't really need to be with people all the time. She could just be peaceful doing her art.

Barbara Cassidy This is my favourite picture. 'The Essence of Eva' I call it, though she
never titled her pictures. She was in her early twenties when she did it. The transparent
figure is her; it is almost like there is a premonition. The figure is admiring the clouds.
Eva was always fascinated with the changing cloud formations. Cedar trees grow wild
here, sometimes roads are lined with them in Maryland. She was so fond of them. She
would actually get out of the car and touch the rough bark. Her senses were always
aware – sight, sound, smells and touch; the blues, the greens – very soothing colours she
chose over and over again in her art-work.

Hugh Cassidy Barbara
calls it 'The Essence of Eva'.
She never called it that; but
we knew it was her. She had a
thing for drawing cedar trees.
We have them out in the
fields and she liked to draw
them. They are in a lot of her
drawings. And there is a little
trademark of hers – she
called it 'the bubble' – some
sort of other-worldly aspect.
Eva's essence is surely there.

THE BABY WITH THE VASE

Hugh Cassidy I like it a lot. I like the cuteness of the boy, but I don't know what he's reaching for. You can see the bubble again and the flower on the floor. It's kind of a puzzling picture, but it works, even with no hand there. She was in the habit of not always finishing some of the pieces that she would do. Other people have told me that she always had her mind full of so many ideas, it was often difficult to know where to begin next.

Barbara Cassidy At the nursery they actually had a rose like that flower. It was called the 'Blue Nile' and it was her favourite – a very pale, lavender-coloured rose. She never would sit at an easel and paint. It all came out of her head and incorporated nature. It could be called a surrealistic painting. I think she was a very, very gifted artist.

THE BOY IN THE NEST

Barbara Cassidy She loved caricatures and drawings. This was a high school project – a pen-and-ink, 'The Boy in the Nest'. She was eighteen at the time.

Hugh Cassidy There's a little bit of a surrealistic element. Note the elfin ears – a little fantasy I guess you'd call it.

Towards the end of 1993, Eva's relationship with Chris came under strain…

Chris Biondo Eva needed to be in control of her life and to have her own place. It had
come to a point where she couldn't continue living with me and fulfil what she needed
to do. I think it was a good thing for her, because I really think she missed out on a lot
of the growing process – of getting your own place and making decisions about doing
things. It was difficult for us to go through that for a while.

Barbara Cassidy He was heartbroken and he said, 'Can't you talk to her?' But they kept
on performing together. He kept on recording and they remained wonderful friends.
She didn't have any regrets, because the relationship continued on a working basis – on
a friendship basis – and then she felt good about it again, once Chris had accepted they
wouldn't get back together. After Chris, the ensuing time was liberating for her. She
thought men were too demanding, too possessive and stifling at times. She used to say,
'When romance gets in the way, it can ruin a friendship.'

Chris Biondo There are people I've been in relationships with that I'd never want to see
again and don't have time for, and then there's Eva. And that's just because she didn't
have a mean bone in her body. People start to fight and do stuff and say terrible things
when relationships end, but we didn't do that kind of thing. We were good friends to
the point where we spent a lot of time making music together. We played gigs and saw
a movie every week. We still went on vacation together and it was good.
Eva and I were different people, if you look at it. I loved to get into spirited conversations
with people and make fun of people I don't like. She preferred to have pleasant
conversations about nature and love everybody.

Margret Cassidy Eva always loved him; it's not that she didn't. But I think that she just
didn't want to make the commitment. I think that she just wanted to live her own life
and not have anyone put demands on her or control her in any way. I just don't think
she had a lot of time to invest in a relationship, because she had not only the music,
but also the art-work and her friends. She had to spend time with our mother, so she
just didn't have the time for a really serious relationship. She wasn't willing to give that
up and I don't blame her. You have to give up a lot of yourself to be with someone else
and I don't think she wanted to do that.

**Eva moved into the spare room of an Annapolis woman, Jackie Fletcher,
whom she had first met two years previously. Jackie was to become one of Eva's
biggest fans and champions…**

Jackie Fletcher The first time I heard Eva sing was in my house at a Christmas party.
As the party wore on, I noticed some people trying to encourage Eva to get up and sing
at a microphone over by the fireplace. She was very reluctant to do so and she had to be
coaxed. Finally she got up to the microphone and she chose *Stormy Monday* and that
was the first time I heard Eva sing live. I was stunned. If you hadn't been looking at her,

you'd think she was a black woman. It was a beautiful, beautiful rendition of *Stormy Monday* and I was so impressed. I thought, 'Damn, what talent does *she* have!'

She came to live with me shortly after she'd broken up with Chris. Things hadn't been working out and she chose to move on and decided to move to Annapolis. I happened to have a room and she called it her 'apartment upstairs'. It was tough for her, because she didn't want to hurt Chris. She wanted Chris to be happy and she wanted Chris to date around, but at the same time that made her nervous.

At this time Eva embarked on a new and challenging phase of her career when she booked a series of solo concerts in small venues in Annapolis. Those who witnessed these performances saw her in her preferred setting: on her own, performing songs of her choice with the arrangements she herself devised…

Jackie Fletcher She started booking herself solo gigs in the Annapolis area and one of the places was Pearl's. It was a beautiful little restaurant with a large mural on the wall, and it had a stage. Eva deliberately went to Pearl's to work on her stage presence and her song selection. She was very clear about that.

The first time she played there she got up on stage and sat with her leggings and her oversized lumberjack shirt and picked up her guitar, and at exactly 8 o'clock started to sing. She never looked up once for two hours and sang non-stop – just one song after another – no eye contact with the audience and no words. The songs were very pretty, very beautiful, very thought-out, but you could tell she was too shy to talk with the audience, or even look at them.

'She came to live with me shortly after she'd broken up with Chris. Things hadn't been working out and she chose to move on and decided to move to Annapolis. I happened to have a room and she called it her 'apartment upstairs'. It was tough for her, because she didn't want to hurt Chris. She wanted Chris to be happy. She wanted Chris to date around, but at the same time that made her nervous.' Jackie Fletcher

Photographed by
her mother, Barbara,
in Nova Scotia.

Barbara Cassidy I went to Pearl's a couple of times. It was a very casual setting, kind
of dark, I think, and she felt really at home. She could eat there on her breaks and she'd
go and fix a sandwich. The Murphys showed up and her supervisor from Behnke's,
David, brought his little daughter. It was mostly friends and friends of friends, word
of mouth.

Hugh Cassidy The crowds who went to hear her at Pearl's were notoriously slim.
The applause on those recordings is sparse, but we were the true believers. We were
the people who wept when she sang and they knew that this kid had the goods.
I saw she was good, but I had no idea how good she really was.

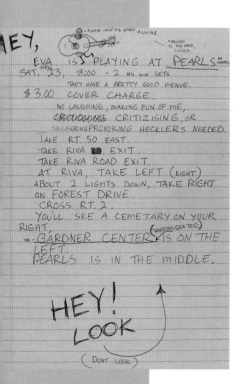

Jackie Fletcher The audience could be anything from seven to thirty, depending on the night. When I knew Eva was playing, I would get on the phone and call everybody in my phone book and try to get them to show up. Eventually we helped Eva get a mailing list together; we passed a pad around and asked people to put their names and addresses and phone numbers on a pad. Her mailing list started there at Pearl's.

Ruth Murphy People loved it. People would cry. It would be pin-drop silence, which is unusual for a restaurant. People did pay attention. People really did appreciate her voice when she would sing and sometimes that would scare her a little bit because, all of a sudden, people are looking at her again.

Barbara Cassidy They were just totally spellbound. *Over the Rainbow* always had a great impact and *Tall Trees in Georgia*, which she loved so much. When she performed in Annapolis and did those ballads, you could see people sitting there, crying. It really went straight to their heart and soul – these old ballads, bittersweet, kind of sad at the end. That stuff really grabbed people. I was very touched and proud at the same time, seeing her up there.

These performances helped build Eva's confidence…

Hugh Cassidy She never embraced her audience. She used other ways of reaching them with her words, her phrasing and the lightness of the melody – the breathiness sometimes of her singing and the gentle strokes on the guitar. They all worked their little mesmerising magic and she didn't have to engage eyeball-to-eyeball.
She'd say, 'Is everybody still awake?' She didn't even know what to say. Often she would run through her songs: bingo, bango, bingo. No patter in between – one beautiful tune after another.

Keith Grimes When it was just Eva, people would feel a great warmth for this person who was expressing things so beautifully and yet it wasn't really that easy to get in, in a way, because there was a part of Eva that was kind of removed. When she was singing the song, she had no trouble bringing out what was inside, but in terms of just relating to the audience, I think that was something that she was still working on.

Ruth Murphy She was scared. She would sometimes forget the notes on the guitar when playing *Over the Rainbow*. She looked as if she was looking at us, but she really was not looking at us. Occasionally she would give you a smile, like if you really made eye contact there.

'If you list all of the songs she recorded and see what they are about — People Get Ready, Golden Thread, Wayfaring Stranger, Over the Rainbow — I think in every case you'll find that they are about transcendence, moving on, taking care of one another, being responsible for your actions, hope, love supreme. They are about the human condition.

Hugh Cassidy

Jackie Fletcher Eventually she learned to look up and after that she learned to talk a little bit and she got more used to people. They became her friends. She would do a set and then she would talk to people and then do another set. So she learned during a break that she could chat a little and get to know these people that were coming every single time, like a fan club. She learned to recognise people when they came in and she could say 'Hi' into the microphone.

Recordings of Eva at Pearl's are evidence of the compelling quality of her performances and demonstrate the range of her song selection and extent of her arranging talents. Songs she regularly performed included Paul Simon's *American Tune*, standards and traditionals, like *Tennessee Waltz* and *A Red, Red Rose* and, perhaps, most impressive, her version of Fairport Convention's *Who Knows Where the Time Goes…*

Barbara Cassidy A song really had to appeal to her, had to have the lyrics, had to have meaning; otherwise she wouldn't have done it. She would have turned it down. Everything had to have a meaning to her and it didn't matter what style music it was. If it appealed to her, she did it.

Jackie Fletcher I think when she sang a song, she thoroughly felt the song and the words. Often people hadn't thought about the words before and when they hear Eva sing, they realise the words have meaning and it strikes them – strikes a chord of sorrow or remembrance of loved ones, or pain, or lost love. Lost love, I think, is a theme that runs through a lot of the songs. Also the theme of dying. Often her songs were about dying and crossing over to the other side.

Hugh Cassidy If you list all of the songs she recorded and see what they are about – *People Get Ready, Golden Thread, Wayfaring Stranger, Over the Rainbow* – I think in every case you'll find that they are about transcendence, moving on, taking care of one another, being responsible for your actions, hope, love supreme. They are about the human condition. They may be melancholy, but that denotes to me a song that's reflective and thought out. Much in life is bittersweet; they are songs with a pulse, with feeling. Her songs give you hope.

By the time Eva was performing at Pearl's, and similar tiny venues in the Washington area, the quality of her voice, the genius of her arranging and the compelling nature of her performance had reached new heights…

Hugh Cassidy I've had letters from people who are singers and they say they sang along with Eva on record. They find out that they run out of breath, or they realise she's holding a note and then making a leap and all these things, and they found them difficult to do. But with Eva it was done effortlessly.

Other people would tell me she was good, too. I didn't trust my own judgment. I always thought that it was fatherly pride, but it confirmed what I suspected. I knew she had a great feel for a tune. I knew she could move people emotionally with her voice at an early age and I think that's her greatest gift. Her words paint a picture and you see it and you feel and you react emotionally to it.

Larry Melton Pearl's is where I think the true Eva was. That's really where she wanted to be, playing quiet ballads. She wasn't fond of loud drummers, but loved brushes. You hear her voice and the little inflections and which would be hidden under a big rhythm section. So that's why she was really going solo. That's where she was heading.

'It was cry, laugh, cry, laugh

and it gave her an opportunity to express

herself the way she needed to.'

Anna Karen Kristinsdottir

Autumn Leaves

Dan Cassidy She loved Iceland. It's a beautiful place – it was a good time. She got on live radio and sang *Bridge Over Troubled Water*. She got followed by fans and there were people coming to hear her every night! It was a very successful little trip.

Barbara Cassidy She performed a couple of nights and she got a write-up on the front page of the newspaper the next morning and had an interview on Icelandic radio. It's a small country! She got all this attention and she loved it.

Iceland came to be a place of some significance for Eva Cassidy. Her younger brother Dan had visited, then settled there in the early 1990s. Recollections of the time she spent there consistently describe the country's liberating effect on her…

Dan Cassidy In 1994, after two years in Iceland, I met the owner of a bar called the Blues Bar in Reykjavik and I thought, 'Hey, Eva could come on up and sing.' I kept telling this bar-owner how good Eva was and eventually she said, 'OK, let's book her and she'll sing every night apart from weekends – see how it goes. I'll pay her flight.' She came over with Mom and Larry Melton.

I hadn't heard her in two years and she sang better than I had ever imagined she would. I was amazed. I shut up and listened and so did everyone else in the audience when she sang those heart-wrenching ballads. She had a little more of a white influence. It wasn't

all about trying to be Aretha Franklin. She was listening to Sinead O'Connor, Annie
Lennox of the Eurythmics, a bluegrass singer named Alison Krauss and a local singer,
Grace Griffith.

Eva was a self-contained act, if she wanted to be, by 1994. Her music was very folk-influenced
with the odd R 'n' B song like *Ain't No Sunshine*. But she always did them as ballads.
Her solo repertoire was almost entirely ballads: Paul Simon tunes, Simon and Garfunkel
tunes, even *Imagine* by John Lennon was in her repertoire.

**In the audience that evening was a young woman, who, though she only knew Eva briefly,
would become as close a friend as any in Eva's life. She offers a unique insight into Eva's
character, frustrations and hopes for the future…**

Dan Cassidy I introduced Eva to my friend, Anna Karen, because Anna Karen was what
Eva would never be: outgoing, chirpy, uninhibited, optimistic and upbeat. She was also a

ABOVE With Dan
in Iceland, 1994.

RIGHT At the Blues
Bar, Reykjavik.

singer. I felt that maybe Eva would like to meet her. Eva loved people unlike her. She
didn't look for people just like her. She picked her friends very carefully and then they
clicked right away. Eva started having fun because these people brought that out of Eva.
It was always in her from being a kid, a fun-loving person, but it had to be brought out
of her – almost coaxed out of her – just through hanging out with upbeat people.
Upbeat people brought her up and lifted her.

Anna Karen Kristinsdottir We were great friends from the beginning. I thought she
was beautiful – her smile – her eyes glowed, but she seemed shy. You could see it in her
eyes. She gave the impression that she was shy, but she was almost bursting with life.
She was shy, but she wasn't shy.

The Blues Bar was the most fun place to perform because you're playing almost inside the group – you're with the audience and she liked that, being close to the audience. People stopped talking when she started singing. There was silence and I got goose bumps the first time I heard her sing. She just threw me off with that voice. I told her and she said, 'Really, you really think so? Thanks.' She was very grateful, but I always got the impression that she didn't believe that people would think that. 'You really think I can sing, you're not kidding me, Anna Karen?' That's the feeling you got.

We were different in that she didn't want to talk on stage. She didn't want to introduce her songs, she just wanted to be able to close her eyes and sing. I talked between the songs, and introduced the songs and got the people to act and dance.

With Anna Karen
in Iceland.

She wanted to be more relaxed in her way of speaking and just say, 'Hey, you guys, is everybody feeling good?' to chat and dance and move, but she just stood there and said, 'Hello everybody,' and didn't look straight at the people.

The nature of Eva's relationship with Anna Karen was closely related to the sense of liberation she experienced in Iceland, two-and-a-half thousand miles from her home. Anna Karen saw a side of Eva rarely seen by others…

Anna Karen Kristinsdottir She was free in Iceland. Nobody knew her. She loved the way we treated her. She came to the house and we made her cocktails and she wanted me to dress her up, and wear jewellery and fancy shoes and a little make-up. She was ready to let go of herself a bit, enjoy herself to the full. There wasn't any criticism and there wasn't any judging. She was just there with her friends and having fun, feeling beautiful and relaxed. We had a lot of fun times in Iceland, going to clubs, meeting guys. She got a lot of attention from the guys. Everybody loved her, she was laughing the whole time.

Emotions got out when we went out, and when she had maybe a cocktail or a liqueur or something. She was among friends, in dark pubs or clubs, and she could open up and be herself and be happy and smiling. The friendship grew and we used to talk about being kindred spirits. She loved being around friends, relaxing among friends and feeling safe.

She wanted me to talk and sing with her – just us. I ran her a bubble bath once and made her a cocktail and gave her a little bottle of perfume. She liked that. She was not afraid to ask for things: 'Let's talk, let's be together just the two of us.' She needed that. She was sometimes too much of a loner and she needed to express herself. She was filled with life and spirit and when you were around her you could feel this energy.

Eva was just a bundle, a wrapped package tied with a bow, bursting with feelings and

Out on the town with Anna Karen and friends in Iceland.

In the wilds, Iceland, 1994.

emotions and views. She was just closed, really closed, but she was trying to open up. She was filled with emotions – fear, anger – and she was trying to get out of that package. She was normal and human like all of us. She just had a hard time expressing herself and sometimes I had to push her to let go. I used to sometimes grab her shoulders and shake her and look in her eyes and say, 'Listen Eva, live, don't be afraid to be happy.'

We were connecting. Sometimes we used to sit and just listen to music or talk. It was cry, laugh, cry, laugh and it gave her an opportunity to express herself the way she needed to, to get rid of the fear of the child. She was just a little girl – a shy, afraid little girl that needed to be hugged. She loved getting hugged and touched. She was afraid though. Sometimes she couldn't give back the hug.

This closeness grew over the course of Eva's two visits to Iceland in the 1990s and regular letter and telephone contact between the two friends. As a consequence, Anna Karen came to understand a great deal about Eva's feelings, about her talent, and the important relationships in her life…

Eva and Barbara in Iceland.

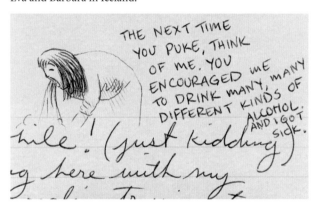

Anna Karen Kristinsdottir She dreaded other people's opinion of her. We talked about that, and she didn't want anybody to be able to say bad things about her. She was a perfectionist and that has a lot to do with her relationship with her father. She wanted to have everything perfect, because she thought that he wanted to have everything perfect.

She was a bundle of all those mixed-up feelings from childhood and teenage years and from all the people she had met through her life. She could be a bit too critical of people. I had to slap her round the hand sometimes and say, 'Eva, don't say that.' And then we talked about it and she would say, 'Yeah, OK, I don't have to be that hard on her or him.'

She told me she loved Chris – loved him to pieces. Eva told me many, many times that it would have been her worst nightmare to lose her friendship with him. She would never have been able to face that, but she never really thought that she could love him and be with him, because she just wasn't ready. Eva just couldn't give him what she wanted to give him and that's why she wanted and needed to get out of that relationship. Eva dreaded losing the friendship. She liked attention from guys. She loved it – I mean, she was a woman – and she got lots of it. Eva wanted to meet guys and, although she was pressing me to have kids, she thought she would probably never have one because she was too immature.

Returning from Iceland in 1995, Eva made some important changes: she left her job at Behnke's to work with a local artist and moved out of Jackie Fletcher's house and found a place of her own in Annapolis…

Jackie Fletcher She stayed with me for less than a year before she started looking around for apartments. She was not having a good time here. She even wrote me a note saying that she didn't want to hurt my feelings, but she needed to live by herself. I liked getting that note, because I think maybe it would have hurt my feelings, so I appreciated that. It was very sweet.

She finally found a little place right down the road and she had to fix it up first before moving in. That took quite a bit of work for her. In exchange for rent, she painted it and cleaned it for one month. She was so happy to be on her own. She cleaned, and she had food there and she got kitty cats and she was very happy. I think that may have been the first time she lived on her own in her entire life. She was thirty-three years old.

In her room
at Jackie's place, 1996.

Hugh Cassidy She had some plans for that little apartment on West Street in Annapolis. It was the first place that she had that was not shared by someone else, which represented a big step. When you have your own place, you can more or less speak from strength – because you're not under my thumb – you never were under my thumb – but if you think you were under my thumb, well, then maybe you were. Our relationship was much better when she had her own place and her freedom. She had to make her own meals and pick up her own socks, and so on and so forth.

Professionally there were also indications that things were moving in a positive direction. Eva had received an award from the Washington Area Music Association and grew in confidence with her solo performances. However, the Blue Note saga was about to reach an unsatisfactory conclusion…

Bruce Lundvall I said, 'Let's see her live, let's audition her.' So I went down to Fleetwood's, in Virginia, a couple of times and I said to her, 'Eva, what do you want to do? Because we are a jazz label, and you have a great, great voice, but you go from *Bridge Over Troubled Water* to *Over the Rainbow*, to a country song, to a rhythm and blues song.' She said, 'Well, I don't wanna be pigeonholed. I just want to sing.'

Chris Biondo I met Bruce Lundvall once. We were playing at Fleetwood's and Mick Fleetwood was there and we were in the dressing room. Mick Fleetwood was really trying to plug her and trying to be supportive and saying he really thought she was good. I went up to Bruce and we were shaking hands and I held onto his hand and looked him right in the eye and I said, 'Bruce, are you going to do anything?' He looked at me and he said, 'Yes, we're going to do something.' So I let go of his hand and that's the only words I ever had with that guy.

Bruce Lundvall I sent two of my guys down there to see her, and I said, 'Look, I think we should just sign her,' but they came back and said, 'Look, she doesn't have a direction. It just doesn't work. She's great, but how are you gonna market her? Where are you gonna take her? How are you gonna go to radio with her? You should just pass. Let it go until she's ready to focus.'
After that it kind of drifted a little, but I was still keeping the door open for Eva because I thought she was brilliant, but I was also thinking: unless she made a jazz record, what was I going to do with her? She was very spiritual, very giving, but a very shy girl. On the other hand she was really persistent about what she wanted, musically.

Mick Fleetwood I used to have long conversations with her, saying, 'Well, maybe you could do this, maybe you could do that,' and the end result was that she used to say, 'Well, if someone doesn't understand why I want to do an interpretation of *Over the Rainbow*, then I don't want to deal with these record companies.' She was true to what she believed in. I wouldn't say she was her own worst enemy, but what I did realise, and really came to respect, was that she didn't want to do anything that really wasn't being true to her art-form, and this was when I gave up trying to give her certain types of advice. It is unusual, because often people kind of bend with the flow a little bit, to make some progress, but she didn't. And it was sort of charming, but it must have been very frustrating for her trying to get someone to accept her for who she was.

Dan Cassidy I personally thought she should, and could easily, have gotten signed by a smaller label, less prestigious, that took acoustic folk singers. She could sell a song through her voice, no matter what she sang. It shouldn't have been a problem getting a contract, but having been on a waiting thing with Blue Note records, how could she even think about that? So we spoke about this and my personal dream was to take her to England, where I knew the scene very well. We could easily have done the folk circuit as a duo, performed up and down Britain, and probably would have run into some very good reviews.

Barbara Cassidy They wanted to place her in some category and she just wouldn't be placed in the category. That's the American music industry for you. It's almost an embarrassment that her voice has to be sent over to England to be successful because her beauty could not be marketed here. They couldn't pigeonhole her. She refused that. And if she couldn't be diverse, she'd rather sing to herself. I don't even know if she took it as a rejection; she never expressed an opinion about disappointment.

Blues Alley was a venue where Eva performed during her time with Chuck Brown, but the significance of a solo Eva Cassidy concert there was considerable. Established in 1965, Blues Alley's reputation as a blues and jazz venue was unparalleled. Eva was never entirely happy with the performance recorded there early in January 1996. The album *Eva Cassidy: Live at Blues Alley* is testament to Eva's power and quality in live performance, particularly

'*She could sell a song through her voice, no matter what she sang. It shouldn't have been a problem getting a contract.*'

Dan Cassidy

on ballads. Her version of Sting's *Fields of Gold,* the Louis Armstrong classic, *What a Wonderful World,* and her version of her childhood favourite, Buffy Sainte-Marie's *Tall Trees in Georgia* are haunting…

Lenny Williams We knew she had a cold and we knew she sounded a lot better on other nights. We were going to do two nights of recording, but we lost the whole first night because of a buzz. A light created a buzz into the tape, so we threw out the whole first night. So everything on the record is one take on the second night, and we knew there was no going back.

Chris Biondo I've heard those songs a million times, so I know that her voice is cold-related. There are some things that she could have done better if she hadn't had a cold, but people still love that record. So just imagine what it would have been like if she'd been firing on all cylinders. She had to do note substitutions for different things because she knew she couldn't hit them. Her voice cracked, she was a little hoarse.

Hugh Cassidy I think there was always that little nagging doubt. She was always nervous before she got up on stage. I remember at Blues Alley, she said she was just as nervous as could be. She wasn't a drinker, but she'd take a shot of vodka, just to take the edge off, and that seemed to work for her. When she started singing she realised that all the fears were groundless. The automatic took over.

Margret Cassidy I went with my parents to see one of the *Live at Blues Alley* shows and I liked how she talked to the audience and then she did that song, *Tall Trees in Georgia,*

Advertisement for
Live at Blues Alley
concert, January 1996.

CHEEK TO CHEEK
BRIDGE
FINE & MELLOW
RT. 66
WONDERFUL W
BLUE SKIES
FEVER
SUMMER TIME
NEXT TIME
AUTUMN LEAVES

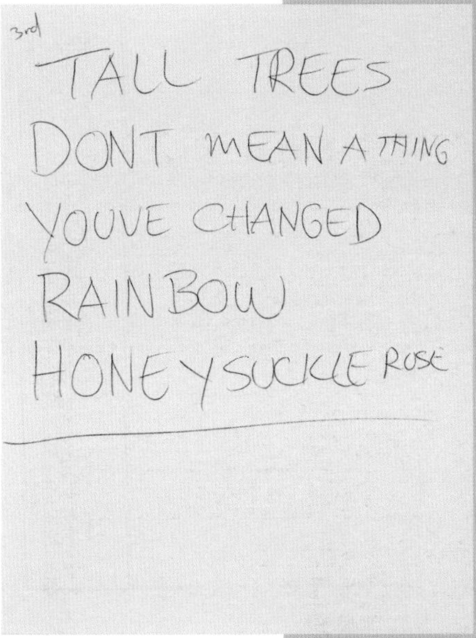

1st

2nd

TALL TREES
DONT MEAN A THING
YOUVE CHANGED
RAINBOW
HONEYSUCKLE ROSE

3rd

Set list for *Live at Blues Alley* concert, January 1996.

'We knew she had a cold and we knew she sounded a lot better on other nights. We were going to do two nights of recording, but we lost the whole first night because of a buzz.

A light created a buzz into the tape, so we threw out the whole first night.

So everything on the record is one take on the second night, and we knew there was no going back.' Lenny Williams

With Anna Karen.

which goes back to Buffy Saint-Marie. I had never heard her do that song before and when I sat in the audience and heard her do that, it was so beautiful that I just cried. Just the guitar work and her voice alone – just those two. It was so beautifully done, it brought tears to my eyes.

Chris Biondo I remember when we played those two nights at Blues Alley. She tried to wear a dress and high heels and, of course, she kicked them off after the first song and said one of the few things she said to the audience, which was, 'I'm never doing this again.' And the next night she came back and was wearing what you see on the *Over the Rainbow* video.

The footage of Eva's performance of *Over the Rainbow* has become famous. It was shot on amateur video by a friend and former work-colleague, Brian McCulley. It is perhaps the best-quality film available of Eva in performance. According to her father, Hugh, it provides evidence of the improvement in Eva's stage performance…

Hugh Cassidy In that grainy film of *Over the Rainbow* there's one point where she looks up and she looks kind of sultry. There's a definite look out at the audience and that's a big change from what she was doing. That, probably more than anything, encapsulates the level she was getting to. Probably if she'd been able to keep on going, she would have related more and become more comfortable in her thing.

There are some singers who can take liberties with a song and she did it with *Over the Rainbow*. She monkeyed with the chord structure and put different chords in there and changed the timing, but she knew where she was going with it. I think that was the most radical change of any song that she did. It's as if she completely disassembled the song and then put it back together. Her voice was richer and smokier. There was more nuance when she got older and those pathways of vocalising were well-greased – she'd sung it so many times between 1984 and 1996.

It's her phrasing that makes you really feel those words. The words were always good, but they got into a casualness that Eva made alive again. With the slower pace and her sure phrasing – she made those words so much more telling. They just come right through and grab the listener in a way that is remarkable.

I know she was aware that her music moved people and brought many of them to tears. I've seen it – it happened at Blues Alley.

When Anna Karen arrived in Annapolis shortly after the Blues Alley recording, Eva voiced doubts about the release…

Anna Karen Kristinsdottir I stayed with her for a few weeks in January through to February 1996. She was playing me the demo of *Blues Alley*. We had a long ride to a gig and she was playing *Fields of Gold* and I said, 'Wouldn't it be great to send a copy of this to Sting?' and she was almost saying, 'What's wrong with you? Are you out of your mind? That would never happen.' I said, 'Well, it could happen. Just make it happen.'

She never believed in her wildest dreams. She said, 'I can't wait to finish that CD' – I'm talking about *Blues Alley* – 'to do stuff that I want to do, the way I want to do it.' She wasn't happy with it. She thought it was too aggressive and not so much her and the way she would have wanted it, and, of course, she was releasing that music and she wanted to be happy with it. But she didn't like that CD. It depressed her. She got mad about it.

Chris Biondo She just said it sucked and that we couldn't do anything with it. 'I don't like it, I don't like it.' I didn't think it sucked. I put it through my studio board and added some reverb and said, 'We'll just do this and it'll sound pretty good. There's like forty songs on here. We'll pick the best ones and if there's something really bad, we'll try to fix it if we can. Let's put it out. I think it'll be really good.' And she started crying. Her face turned red – tears poured out of her eyes.

She said, 'Can I put *Golden Threads* on it?' I said, 'Sure,' and she said, 'I'll do it if we get to finish the record I'm working on.' And I said, 'We're going to finish it anyway, it's no big deal.' So we mixed the record and I think she felt a little bit better about it. She was real excited the day we picked the record up and I couldn't believe it. The reviews of *Live at Blues Alley* were better than any records I've ever seen. Everybody said it was great, fantastic, obviously amazed with how many styles Eva was doing – how good her voice was. *Fields of Gold* was on that record and that was a pretty popular song.

Hugh Cassidy   She critiques many of her songs on *Blues Alley* because of having a cold that time; but as Chris Biondo said, what most people don't realise is that Eva with a cold is better than most with their regular voice.

Dan Cassidy   Her music was leaning more towards acoustic guitar and after she'd recorded *Blues Alley* she wrote to me in a letter dated May 12th 1996 saying: 'I am already very aware of all the mistakes, being very critical, and I am my own worst critic and I have never needed Dad or anyone to tell me what is bad or wrong. This recording was incredibly stressful. We were having technical difficulties. My voice was in bad shape. It always is like that in the winter. I prefer studio recording, I am so tired of competing with loud guitars and drums and I'm tired of singing R 'n' B and blues. I'm really heading in the folk direction, yeah, folk with influences of any beautiful music, I'm sick of shouting. You will be laughing at how out-of-tune the guitars are on *Fields of Gold*.'

Dan Cassidy   She was struggling financially over *Live at Blues Alley* too, she wrote: 'I spent about $4,000 on this CD. My Aunt Isabel was kind and donated $1,000, but CD, taxes, dental work – two root canals and crown – new apartment, car insurance, has taken away all my savings and almost all of my credit card limit. But I'm still afloat – knock on wood. Now I hope I can sell all my CDs and tapes and be doing OK.'

On the sleeve of *Live at Blues Alley* Eva thanks her parents 'for giving me love and a deep appreciation of music', a dedication which echoes her introduction to *What a Wonderful World*:
'I'd like to dedicate this song to my Mom and Dad. They're here tonight. Dad taught me how to play guitar…'
This dedication was evidence of an improvement in Eva's relationship with her father, which, by his own admission, had not been as close as he would have wished…

Hugh Cassidy   We're too much alike? I suppose there's something to be said for that. It was funny when I heard her say, 'And my Dad taught me to play guitar.' It sort of just lays out on the air like that. I think she wanted to add something, but then lost her thought midway. And that's why that sounds so strange. I didn't think too much about it, but I was surprised that she said it. It came out just spontaneously. I think she was trying to give me some pleasure by mentioning that I helped her, and I received it well. The relationship was good. She felt better about herself. You know, the better you feel about yourself – both parties, no matter who – the more accommodating you can be towards each other. So if she feels she's at a good place and I feel I'm at a good place, you have a good day. We had some good moments and we were getting back together. By then she had her own little apartment and she could say, 'This is my place and these are my rules,' and not feel belittled, which I think she felt more keenly than others when she hadn't a place for herself. We were getting a good handle on it. I had severely wrenched my back that month and she

'It was funny when I heard her say, "And my Dad taught me to play guitar." It sort of just lays out on the air like that. I think she wanted to add something, but then lost her thought midway. And that's why that sounds so strange.'

Hugh Cassidy

offered to take me out and drive me around the countryside. We both loved the outdoors and the sun on our backs and she was feeling good about herself. She had her apartment.

While Eva always knew her own mind, there were clear signs that by 1996 she was translating this into a real vision for her music and finding a way to articulate it in the studio…

Keith Grimes When she did something on acoustic guitar, basically she'd just come in and she'd have the whole arrangement. I mean the band would add to that, but the skeleton of the arrangement was already there. She'd come in with an arrangement that worked for her and she was comfortable with. She had an arranger's sense that enabled her to play things that were very appropriate to the songs, and she had enough technique to pull off what she wanted to do. For the things that she couldn't do, I was there. Lucky for me!

Larry Melton She was making a lot of progress, I think she loosened up a lot. I think a lot of people mistake shyness for just being a quiet, mellow person, sitting and playing a guitar – like what are you going to do, tell jokes? That's the nature of her music. I don't think she was necessarily so inhibited and shy, it was just quiet, mellow music. I get a little tired of hearing, 'Oh, she was so shy.' It was just the nature of the ballads and stuff.

Hugh Cassidy She liked brushwork and percussion, but not the heavy, loud drums that she had to sing over. There are some notable exceptions in some of the work that's been done. When Lenny Williams plays the piano on *Autumn Leaves* and Keith Grimes plays guitar fills on *Wayfaring Stranger*, they are just beautiful. But largely she could carry it by herself. Her selection of chords, her timing, she and her guitar as one unit – that's what she was thinking of doing: a solo career.

Barbara Cassidy I think she finally set goals for herself. She wanted to go out and sing, just her and her guitar. She wanted to improve her life and do what was really good for Eva. She finally grew up and wanted to be an independent person and act independently.

Chris Biondo She was getting there with the songs she was doing and was a person who would have been a magnificent producer. She got the whole music thing. She understood how to come up with the idea for a style to play a song and relay it to the people that she was working with and she was asserting herself.

I remember she was talking about *Wayfaring Stranger*. She came off the subway and said,
'I had a great idea. I want to do *Wayfaring Stranger*. I want to have Keith play guitar like
Wes Montgomery and I want you to play this bass line.' She handed me the bass line.
'And I want the drums to play this kind of old R 'n' B-style of thing with the brushes and
stuff and I want Rhodes electric piano, like Ray Charles would play.' And we all came in
and she pointed and hummed and that was so cool to see. Left on her own she could have
really, at some point down the road, completely achieved everything she wanted.

Hugh Cassidy She really wanted to travel in Europe one day and just live the life of a
wanderer and play her music. She said, 'I've got the easiest job in the world. All I've got
to do is sing and play guitar.' That's what she would have liked to have done. She had no
real aspirations for having fame, but she had definite plans on what she wanted to do:
doing art when she wished, doing music when she wished and to have the freedom to
have her days free to go out in the countryside and partake of nature.

Anna Karen Kristinsdottir The singing, guitar, going abroad, coming to Iceland –
that was what she was going to do. She was going to spend the trip there singing just

with her guitar. Singing was a drug, it made her relax, it made her loosen up and it made her get rid of the fears and the anger and unlock that child – that happy, little tiny, fragile person that she was.

Anette Cassidy When my daughter Sarah was born, she and Mom would come to visit. I probably saw more of Eva then than I ever had. I always thought Eva was a kid at heart. She could really find joy in simple things and would have so much fun with Sarah just playing. Sarah has some very fond memories of the times that she spent together with Eva. They just really connected.

We had time together and it's always been hard for me to open up to anybody. I'm a very private person and most of the time keep my thoughts to myself. But I remember we really talked in Virginia at my house one night, sitting out on the porch swing. She remembered so many things about our childhood that I didn't. She remembered us going out and picking blackberries near the house in Oxon Hill. She remembered me taking her with me sometimes and letting her ride the ponies. I'd never realised how much she enjoyed spending time with me doing things like that. She really made me feel special when she told me that as we sat out there for several hours. We just talked and talked and it was the first time we had and it might have been the last.

February 2nd, 1996 was Eva's 33rd birthday…

Anna Karen Kristinsdottir We held a surprise party. We put up Happy Birthday ribbons for her and we brought a cake with icing saying 'Happy Birthday Eva', and friends came over and we played music and we had fun. We had helium balloons and she inhaled helium and she started singing. She sang and there were lots of people around and she was making everybody laugh and she was like, 'Everybody's watching

Eva on her
33rd birthday,
2nd February 1996.

me and laughing,' but she enjoyed it. She was loving it. The phone rang, and she'd just inhaled helium, and it was her boss and she was like, 'Hello, yeah, no, I'm sorry, it's helium.' And then it faded off – that was just one of hundreds of funny moments with her.

She took tiny steps – tiny steps towards the point where she was able to open up and be herself and she was always reminding herself to do that. She kept saying to me when we talked that she was working on it. 'Anna Karen, I've been working on it today and I'll get there; and you'll see, Miss Anna Karen!' She was going to come to Iceland. She was going to stay with me for two weeks and we were going to have a blast. We had all kinds of stuff planned and she saw a bright future ahead, being able to open up a bit more – express herself a bit more – meet more people – be in love and be loved.

Barbara Cassidy's recollections of a walk she took with Eva in May of 1996 indicate her daughter's happiness with her life and the modest but growing success she was achieving in her career…

OPPOSITE June 1996, Eva's last outing with her mother.

Barbara Cassidy We were walking in the neighbourhood and talking and she said, 'You know, Mom, I wouldn't have any regrets if I were to die now. I've lived such a full life and I have always been allowed to create.' I think to me that showed she was content; you know, she could do what she really needed to do. She was well known in the Washington area and she had fans in Iceland, Nova Scotia and Germany. Everything was spreading by word of mouth and she was quite happy with that.

'She was well known in the Washington area and she had fans in Iceland, Nova Scotia and Germany. Everything was spreading by word of mouth and she was quite happy with that.' Barbara Cassidy

'I heard her sing Danny Boy and all the

men at the concert were in tears.'

Maggie Haven

What a Wonderful World

In July 1996 it all seemed to be coming together for Eva Cassidy. She was using her artistic gifts working with an artist, Maggie Haven, painting murals in the cafeterias of local schools, and she was collaborating with Chris Biondo on the recordings that would be released as the album *Eva by Heart*. Her new boss was also a fan…

OPPOSITE Mural painted by Eva at Anne Arundel School.

Maggie Haven The beauty of the job was that she got to paint and I was extremely flexible. I knew that music had to come first with her, before the day job. I think she was starting to believe it when we were saying, 'You're great, you're wonderful, by yourself, your stuff, what you're doing.' She would see the reaction. I heard her sing *Danny Boy* and all the men at the concert were in tears. Now, that had to impact her to some extent. I think it was starting to maybe dawn on her that people did really enjoy it.

Eva's new job was absorbing and, in its way, physically demanding…

Maggie Haven One day she said, 'My hip is starting to bother me. I'm sore.' So we talked and we kind of speculated. 'I wonder if it's standing on a ladder,' because if you stand on a ladder all day and you turn at a right angle, you end up putting all your weight on one hip while you're painting, and when you're painting you can get tense. You get so engrossed in what you're doing that a long time can go by and you're remaining in that position. You don't think about it because you're so focused on what you're doing. Shortly after that, my hip was getting sore too, I said, 'Why don't you go to the doctor, find out what the deal is?' So she went to the doctor and she said, 'Well, the doctor thinks it must be some kind of a strain or a sprain because of the ladder work.' She drove for half-an-hour to tell me that she couldn't work that day, because the doctor had just put her on crutches.
She's still doing gigs at this time and she's still painting. I mean, she came in that day and then

after that I would just have her paint, but stay off the ladder. She didn't want to sit home alone and think about it. She liked being in there.

She was on crutches and she was in such pain I went to what I think was her last gig, and that was the saddest thing. She was substituting for a fellow singer who was ill. Just a few of us found out about this gig a few hours before the performance. It was in a sports bar in Annapolis and it was a horrible place. You walk in and there are all these big machines, big huge bar, people sitting around the bar and all these sports games and video games and things. Around the other side of the bar was a little area where she sat, then behind her were all the pool tables. It was an enormous place. The place was packed, mobbed with people. I'd never been in such a place before. So she came in, she was on her crutches and we helped her bring in her stuff. She sat on a stool and sang several songs and there was all this noise going on; there was such a din, I think a lot of people probably didn't really hear her. She would play a tune and we would clap and she would turn to us and say, 'Thank you table number one,' and then laugh.

There was one person whom we all noticed who was directly behind her, way in the back. This guy was an attendant, I think, for the pool tables. He was absolutely turned to stone and he was looking at Eva and he was listening, and he 'got' her. You could tell. He did not move whenever she started to sing. He was listening, but I don't think anybody else was. Afterwards she just said, 'Oh well, so I get my money.'

Hugh Cassidy The strain of being on the ladder was what she felt caused the discomfort in her hip and that was quite a logical assumption. She thought that the hip problem was indeed from being twisted about like that. It didn't heal. Normally after three or four days it should come around and it didn't. So this went on for a week and a half, maybe longer, maybe two weeks.

Barbara Cassidy Eva and I had a plan to go to Nova Scotia again that summer but her hip was hurting. I wanted to go for ten days and I already had my ticket. I said, 'Eva, do you want me to stay home?' and she insisted that we go. In the interim her pain got so much worse. At the back of my mind, when the hip problem happened, I thought: 'I hope this is not a connection with the cancer.'

Chris Biondo She called her sister Anette because she'd fallen in the bathroom and she called me because her parents were out of town. I drove over to Eva's house, put her in the car and got her a wheelchair. Anette and I took her to the park, walked her around a bit and then took her back to the house. The next day we made an appointment. She had an X-ray that said that her hip was busted.

Anna Karen Kristinsdottir She was going to come for a visit. Then she called and said that she might have to delay the trip because they were finding something. Her hip was giving her problems. I remember very vividly that we were joking about her holding her equipment. But I also remember being afraid and I could hear her being afraid, but we joked about it saying: 'You and your heavy stuff.' She always did that – filled the car with equipment and she carried it by herself. So we were hoping that was it.

Barbara Cassidy Arrangements were made for her to get that hip fracture repaired and here in the United States it's customary, before you have any type of surgery, that you get a chest X-ray. I went with her when the X-ray was taken; but it took, I think, an afternoon for them to give her physician her results.

Anette Cassidy I went with her to that later appointment. It was just the two of us and I kept grilling the doctor. I said, 'What kind of prognosis is there?' and I remember the look in his eyes more than what he said.

Barbara Cassidy After that appointment I wasn't home and she came over. She told her father that they had found a spot on the lungs that was cancerous and her first thought was: 'How is Mom going to take this?'

Margret Cassidy I was living in the apartment upstairs at my parents' house in Bowie. I had been living there for a while. I came downstairs and my mother had this worried look on her face. I said, 'What's wrong?' and she just busted out crying and said, 'They did an X-ray on Eva and they found a spot on her lung.' She was really upset, really crying and that got me to crying and I hugged her real hard and said, 'Oh Momma, it's going to be alright, it's going to be alright.' But there was no consoling her. So maybe she knew more than I did. I didn't feel it was hopeless, I still felt hopeful.

Barbara Cassidy Anette, Hugh and I, before the hip surgery in Johns Hopkins, had a consultation with the oncologist. They had done further tests and discovered that the cancer really had spread. He was being very gentle, but at the same time didn't hide any facts. We were numb. None of us had expected such bad news. We were just totally overwhelmed.

He suggested hip repairment right away and then some aggressive treatment. We decided, right there at that first meeting, to go ahead with the aggressive chemotherapy treatment, because that was like a last straw – that was the only hope we had.

Hugh Cassidy   She got the diagnosis and Eva asked point blank, 'What will happen if I don't do anything with it, if I have no treatment?' The doctor said, 'Well, you'd have three or four months to live.' 'And if I do have treatment?' and he said, 'Well, we can't guarantee anything,' but it was implied that treatment would at least give a better fighting chance than non-treatment. She took it very calmly, she was a trooper. Of course, there's no knowing what went on inside; that's not always fully revealed – she kept that private.

I felt that the idea of the treatment was giving her hope. We were addressing it and despite the gravity of the situation, she had hope of getting better and expressed that to me and to us. I think it was very important that she had that hope.

Anette Cassidy   There was some question in her mind, I think, of whether she wanted the chemo – whether she wanted radiation. She asked me what she should do, and you can't tell someone else what they should do. We just talked and I tried to just give her as much information as I could, so that she could make her own decision. Eventually she said, 'I want to live – I want to try this. If there's any possibility I could get better, I've got to try it,' and she hung onto that. Without chemo it would have been a matter of a couple of months, and with the chemo, hopefully she would go into remission, but maybe live for six more months. Remission was what we were hoping for.

Eva's melanoma, first detected in 1993, had spread. Melanoma is a very serious form of skin cancer caused by over-exposure to ultraviolet radiation. The main source of ultraviolet radiation is sunlight and those, like Eva, with blonde hair and fair skin are at especially high risk. The cancer begins in the melanocytes – cells that make the skin pigment called melanin – and when it spreads, or metastasises, cancer cells are also found in the lymph nodes and, as in Eva's case, in other parts of the body, including the lungs or brain. Eva's skin cancer was metastatic melanoma. The extent of the cancer in Eva's body became clearer when tests were carried out at Johns Hopkins Hospital, where she had been admitted for surgery on her fractured hip…

Hugh Cassidy   It was approximately three years later from her mole removal when it all hit home. Evidently this growth had been carrying on all this time and had gotten into her bones. She had the recurring sore hip and in actuality it was severed! I mean, can you imagine walking around with a severed hip? Severed ? That just blows my mind.

Anette Cassidy   The original site was on her back and then we don't know the exact progression. We know it went into her bones and that was what was causing the hip pain. Mom had mentioned the original problem to me once and asked me to please talk to Eva to try to get her to go to her follow-up appointments and I did that. I tried. But she just absolutely hated going to doctors and felt like she was fine and didn't want to deal with it.

Barbara Cassidy   Apparently with the melanoma, it has roots internally and it just spreads and it gets into the bones, into the lungs and even later on they found a spot in her skull. And it destroys the bone. That's why the fracture occurred.

'There was some question in her mind, I think, of whether she wanted the chemo — whether she wanted radiation. She asked me what she should do, and you can't tell someone else what they should do. We just talked and I tried to just give her as much information as I could, so that she could make her own decision. Eventually she said, "I want to live. I want to try this. If there's any possibility I could get better, I've got to try it," and she hung onto that. Without chemo it would have been a matter of a couple of months, and with the chemo, hopefully she would go into remission, but maybe live for six more months. Remission was what we were hoping for.'

Anette Cassidy

Chris Biondo They did a hip replacement on her and I talked to the nurse at Johns Hopkins, who said it was all up and down her spinal cord and in her brain and in her shoulder, in her lungs, in her hip. That's a lot of cancer and when she found out she was sick, it had to be terrifying. I'm sure I saw fear.

Dan Cassidy It was a huge shock. I'd just come off my holiday in England and my Dad left a message saying: 'Give us a call.' I couldn't get through to my parents, so I called Larry, who told me, 'Well, Eva's having problems; they say she has cancer.' I said, 'Well, how serious is the prognosis?' He said, 'You'd better talk to your parents.' He didn't want to tell me. He knew.
An hour later Anna Karen called me. She wasn't getting through to Eva. The second she said, 'Well, they say she only has a few months; she's dying,' that wrecked me. I couldn't eat for a while. It was very bad. That was the worst of it, the initial shock. When you come to terms with something a little more, it hurts, but you can get through the day at least. You can do things and you can make arrangements and make plans and decide: 'How would I like this to be and what can I do for Eva?' I knew I had to go back to see her.

Hugh Cassidy The root of the problem was going sleeveless and bare-headed and bare-necked in the sun. Too many hours, too long a time. She was with the outdoor crew for over eight years. I think her pale skin had something to do with it as well.

Chris Biondo In America kids get sunburnt. Nobody thinks anything of it. They think, 'First sunburn of the year and then you get your tan and you'll be fine.' We did a lot of snorkelling where she had her head in the water and her back was being beaten by the sun. That could have been it too.

When Eva was admitted to Johns Hopkins Hospital for hip surgery, her friends rallied around…

Jackie Fletcher So she had hip surgery and during her recovery at the hospital, her spirits were very good. She had many, many visitors and Johns Hopkins wasn't used to this. So we had to stagger our visiting so we didn't all come at once. Eva provided crayons and paper for everybody and, as we sat out in the hall waiting for our turn to go in, we drew pictures for Eva because that was her requirement. We couldn't come in and visit her unless we drew a picture. So her hospital room was filled with pictures – wall-to-wall. Some people hadn't picked up a crayon in years, but they were required to draw a picture for Eva.

Ruth Murphy I loved going to the hospital to see her. We would take her things and she always had a room full of stuff. There were people sitting down on the floor and they'd all be drawing and we'd collect the pictures. We talked about what she wanted to do now that she knew she had cancer. She said to me that she was going to fight it. But I looked at her – I'm like, 'Eva, you're going to fight this?' and she said, 'Yeah, I decided

I'm going to fight it.' But I really didn't believe that. That just wasn't her nature. She was just not a fighter over that kind of stuff at all and I think it showed. 'OK, I've resigned myself; it's over,' Eva said.

Eva was very happy in her small apartment on West Street in Annapolis. It had been her first entirely independent home. However, after her hip surgery and with the prospect of chemotherapy, she had to make a tough decision about where, realistically, she should live. Her decision marked the beginning of a period where her family – particularly her mother, father and sister Anette – became her care-givers…

Barbara Cassidy She had just moved into that little apartment in Annapolis and it was so attractive the way she had set it up. She was so proud, and she had gotten two kittens, but we insisted she could no longer live there. So she moved back home and she was so hoping she could recover from the surgery. I think she still didn't realise how serious this all was.

Hugh Cassidy We had to empty her apartment and move her home where she could have the family care for her. That day we had to move out all her furniture, all of her friends came by and helped her. We took her stuff out and boxed-up her records. She'd just moved in, I don't know, six, nine months before.

It was heart-rending having to take everything out of her little apartment – to bundle that up and bring it back here and store her stuff in the basement – to realise in your heart of hearts that she may not come out of this, that this was it. On the other hand, there was a part of me that felt that she may recover and wanted to recover and I wanted to be around to help her do that.

Anette Cassidy She knew that she needed to move back home, at least for the time being, and she was OK with it. The way I put it to her was, I said to her, 'You know after this is over you can get your own place again. This is just a temporary set-back.' Part of me believed it. A huge part of me had to believe it. Maybe it was me trying to make myself feel better about the whole thing.

A lot of the time we spent together after then was focused on her illness. I am a registered nurse and I was there with her. The medical language isn't always easy for the layman to understand, and I was there to guide her through the process and explain things to her when she didn't understand what the doctor was saying to her. She looked to me to help her to make decisions as far as her medical care. I went with her to Johns Hopkins. I still lived four hours away and worked every other weekend. On my weekends off I was up there with her – wanting to spend as much time as I could with her and it was all so incredibly hard.

Chemotherapy involves anti-cancer drugs, usually injected or given by mouth – that travel through the bloodstream and attack cancer cells. Chemotherapy drugs will also kill some normal cells and the side effects of the treatment Eva received included nausea and vomiting, loss of appetite and hair loss…

'She lost her hair and it made her nauseated, no appetite. It was the combination of the disease and the treatment and she just got weaker and weaker and was able to do less and less for herself. But she never gave up. She was always there trying, and on her good days she would be up and rallying and would have friends come over and they'd sing.' Anette Cassidy

Barbara Cassidy She had always been so proud of her beautiful hair and the nurse said: 'About a week after your first treatment, your hair will start falling out.' So Maggie gave her a short haircut and we put her hair in a braid and that was a devastating moment for me – her beautiful hair! I had to get away. Then the hair did start falling out and she was so brave. She said, 'Dad, get your shaver and shave it all off.'

Anna Karen Kristinsdottir We talked, like a few phone calls, and we were making jokes about the wig and cutting her hair off and me helping her find different types of wigs and she was saying: 'We're going to have fun doing that.'

Chris Biondo She wasn't a complacent patient. She was very anxious to go to her radiation and chemotherapy. I don't know if I would react like she did, which was very bravely. She really had a lot of class the way she handled her sickness that I don't think I would have had. I mean, she was taking everything they could give her medically and all that stuff makes you sick and it's painful. There's needles; there's vomiting.

Hugh Cassidy Sometimes on these rides home from the hospital, just the action of the car on Baltimore's bumpy streets would just jolt through her body. I'd have to drive very slowly through the city so she wouldn't feel this discomfort. She tried to do some physical therapy at the swimming pool. She studiously would do her little laps in the pool, where the water would help support her and she could walk. She worked hard trying to get her fitness back. I had hopes that she was going to get better – that I was going to be a key figure in helping her to get better. I wanted to wait on her hand and foot and get a bond going. Sometimes that bonding is only done when one or the other of the two parties are helpless. So then, you have to swallow a little bit of whatever pride the members have and seek to accommodate each other. We're talking life and death here. My thinking was that we would go through this together and we would mend our relationship as well, and take it to a new height – because there's nothing greater than to have a daughter or a son that you can have as a friend and do things with – not as a father-daughter – just as a friend to do things with across the generations. That's what I was aiming for. It's not a relationship easily come by and kids can be pretty tough on parents – saying, 'You should've done this.' But I had always envisioned her getting better and my being instrumental in her recovery and I looked at it that way.

Anette Cassidy She lost her hair. The treatment made her nauseated. No appetite. It was the combination of the disease and the treatment and she just got weaker and weaker and was able to do less and less for herself. But she never gave up. She was always there trying, and, on her good days, she would be up and rallying and would have friends come over and they'd sing.

On her visits to Johns Hopkins to receive her chemotherapy, Eva befriended four other young people with cancer, named Kimberley, Kirsten, Daniel and Bruce…

Barbara Cassidy She was close to Kimberley especially, because she had been through it already. Eva later consulted her on the phone about how to deal with the side effects of chemo, what to do. And Daniel was a fine musician. He was a cellist with the Baltimore symphony. Eva gave him a CD and he had made a CD, so they exchanged. Then, at one time, Eva was getting her treatment and Daniel and Kimberley were there and they were just these three wonderful people dealing with their cancer and I was in the background. It's amazing the sense of humour they had, their own brand of humour going through something like that.

Hugh Cassidy They were all her age, in their early 30s. They were all suffering from various types of cancer. They met each other when they were undergoing treatment, so it was several times a week sometimes. And as frequently happens when you're in the same boat, you make friends with your fellow boatmen. So she did that and learned about the lives of these other folk. They had their own little camaraderie and jokes about getting the needle and feeling bloated and dizzy. Sadly, all have since passed away.

Despite her serious illness Eva still hoped to return to the studio to complete her work…

Barbara Cassidy She still had it in her mind, you know. 'I can still go into the studio and record.' And they tried but she was so weak. She just deteriorated so fast after July that she couldn't even hold her guitar up for any length of time.

Chris Biondo I picked her up once and she was too sick. I laid her on the couch, put a microphone in front of her and she tried to play and it was terrible. She was throwing up all the time. She couldn't eat. She was real thin and weak. She was so morphined-out. I told her, 'The thing that scares me most is you've got so much morphine, and you have to because of the pain. I'm scared that you may not be able to have enough energy.' I would imagine if you start falling into the sick-thing there's a certain point that you can't go back from, and I saw that happening. But I knew there was nothing Eva could do about it.

A Tribute to
Eva Cassidy

The Bayou
Tuesday, September 17
doors open at 7pm
$20

(100% of admission price goes to Eva)

featuring:
Pieces of a Dream, Deanna Bogart, Mary Ann Redmond,
Tommy Lepson & the Lazyboys, Chuck Brown, Al
Williams, Keter Betts, Ron Holloway, Jr Cline & the
Recliners, Meg Murray, John Previti, Rich Chorne, Kevin
Johnson, Dave Elliott Band and many others...

As you may or may not know, Eva is currently fighting
cancer. Come celebrate with us her contribution to our
lives and show your support!

The Bayou is located at 3135 K St, NW in Georgetown
The Bayou: (202) 333-2897
Tickets are available at the Bayou or through Ticketmaster

```
BU0917E   THE BAYOU IN GEORGETOWN
A 20.00      3135 K STREET, N.W.
CA 3.25          PRESENTS
GENADM      EVA CASSIDY TRIBUTE
752X  1    *PROOF OF AGE REQUIRED*
GA3  45   TUE SEP 17.1996 DOORS 7PM
OTR1623   CN64526 GENERAL ADMISSIO
17SEP6    GENADM GA3  45   20.00
   DATE SOLD   SECTION  ROW/BOX  SEAT   PRICE (TAX INCL)
```

At the end of September, Eva's friends organised a
concert in her honour at The Bayou club in Georgetown,
Washington DC…

Barbara Cassidy It was arranged as a benefit concert. The news
had spread that Eva didn't have any medical insurance, but that
wasn't true, thank God. Chris Biondo had arranged that some time
previously she had decent medical insurance.

Hugh Cassidy A couple of her friends got together and said,
'Look, Eva's having some problems and we ought to do a benefit
in her honour.' I don't know how it got out that she didn't have
health insurance – she had health insurance – all I knew was there
was something in her honour. It was also very much a social
outpouring of people who wanted to support one of their fellow
musicians.

Jackie Fletcher It was late September 1996, and it's a big
place, but the place was packed. Everybody that could make it
showed up. Finally, after several hours, Eva pulls up outside and
a lot of us came out to see her arrive. I hadn't seen her in a few
weeks and I was so surprised to see how much weight she had
lost, just since the time when I had last seen her. But she still had
stamina and strength and she came out of the car and she had a
walker to help her walk. She was totally bald, but she had a little
hat on and she was smiling from ear to ear, and she was so happy
to see all these people.

Barbara Cassidy All these wonderful groups performed.
Then Eva's band came on stage at maybe ten, ten thirty. I still don't know to this day how
she got the energy, just physically, to get onto the stage. She walked there with her walker.
People were there to carry her, but she said, 'No, I can do it' – and I was right behind her
and people moved – oh, there was a crowd. The place was packed – a space opened up.

Keith Grimes We really didn't know if Eva was going to sing. The band came out and
played, and we backed Chuck Brown for a couple of songs. Then Eva got up there
and I think we did two songs. We did *Red Top*, which is on *The Other Side*. We hadn't
really planned it. We said, 'What are we going to do?'– so somehow we picked that,
which was mainly a Chuck feature, but she said, 'Good, I don't have to sing much on that.'

Jackie Fletcher There were some more discussions and Chuck was breaking up and
getting very emotional. He was so upset. I think he left the stage.

Hugh Cassidy Eva had to be lifted up on her stool to sing. She said she hadn't played the guitar in six weeks or a couple of months, but she thought she could still handle it. She made a couple of self-deprecating jokes regarding her runny nose, which is characteristic when you take morphine. She said, 'Has anyone got a hanky? I guess you've all seen snot before. It's no big deal.' And she mentioned that she was loaded up on morphine. But she said, 'That's OK, all we musicians do anyway is take drugs.' And she laughed and the audience laughed with her, and then she sang *Wonderful World*.

Chuck Brown *What a Wonderful World*. That was the last song she sang the night at The Bayou. It was the last one that she sang. I couldn't sing with her that night. All I could do was sit on the stage there and support her.

Chris Biondo She did *What a Wonderful World* and from the point when she started singing it to maybe ten minutes after she stopped, it was the most surreal experience I've ever had, because it encompassed so much emotional energy all being focused at one person and it was so good. She sang well. She still had the good Eva stuff, and didn't miss a beat. It's like seeing a movie, the best part of a happy movie, or some beautiful bitter-sweet ending-thing, but it was real and we were all there and she got to see that, and I don't think too many people get to see that stuff in their lifetime, tributes or that level of appreciation. I know that it made her happy. I don't think you can go to something like that and have seven hundred people there – there for the sole purpose of showing their love and respect – and not be completely moved and feeling good about yourself, because most people die first and then these things happen. So that was a very, very cool thing.

Eva's thank you card sent to those who helped her during her illness.

Barbara Cassidy They were just sitting stock still, listening to this, and getting so emotional. There wasn't a dry eye. She felt like, 'I'm having a big birthday party.' She felt so tickled that all these people cared to show up. It really lifted up her spirits.

Thank you for thinking of me, and helping to lift my spirits. I love you.

And God bless you a million times over.

Hugh Cassidy She had a lovely time – the outpouring of everyone's sentiments towards her. Then we drove her back home. She said it was a good evening and she was adamant about singing that song, *Wonderful World*, and that was her last public performance.

Ruth Murphy She said she felt the most amazing feeling from the audience. She said, 'They loved me.' And I'm like – 'It took you this long to figure it out Eva?' That was a true, true love that she felt. That was cool.

'She had the magic — the thing that goes

beyond being a really wonderful, creative artist.'

Bruce Lundvall

Over the Rainbow

By October, just three months after her diagnosis, it was clear that there was no real prospect of Eva's cancer going into remission. Increasingly, she was confined to bed in a downstairs room of the family home…

Anette Cassidy She had deteriorated so much yet she just went ahead and finished the round of chemo that she was scheduled for. She was going to continue, but she wasn't totally herself. She was becoming confused at times and my parents pretty much took over making the decisions for her. She always said that she wanted to try everything to get better, but there did come a point where it was obvious that it wasn't going to happen. I think the decision not to continue was made mutually by the doctors, our parents, and probably Eva.

Elaine Stonebraker The last time I saw her was just a couple of weeks before she died. The illness had progressed very rapidly and she was mostly confined to her bed or a wheelchair. In an attempt to try to recall some of our happier times on our bikes, I asked her where she'd like to be if she had her choice. With little hesitation, she answered that she wished she could be lying in the tall grass beside the canal, just south of Olde Town where she had once taken a nap years ago.

Hugh Cassidy It was mainly days in bed and, of course, at the end she never got out of that bed. I had thought we'd be able to talk about it, but she wasn't ready to and then by the time that we could do some real soul-searching, she was unable to communicate. She was so weak and so tired out and in the throes of the drugs, which she needed because the pain required more frequent dosages. So it got to the point where she could no longer ask for pieces of ice to put on her tongue. That's all she wanted at the end, ice, big chunks of ice to chew on to get rid of that dryness.

I was grateful to be allowed to help, to give her food and morphine. She'd be laying there in her bed and I'd offer to rub her feet. She'd be tired and I'd say, 'Eva? Do you mind if I rub your feet for a little bit?' and she'd say, 'Well, OK, but just for a little bit,' as if she's saying, 'Yeah if that's what you must do to feel better and everything, then you can go ahead and rub my feet.' It was something I was trying to do for her, not out of guilt, but because I loved her and when she'd say, 'Well, alright, but just for a little bit,' I'd keep going till she'd fall asleep. She had this kind of independent streak until the end. A lot of us have trouble giving and receiving love. It's a thing you go through your life learning.

Eva's brother, Dan, returned home from Iceland to see his sister while there was still time…

Dan Cassidy Anna Karen and I flew back to see Eva. She was in a wheelchair at that time and she was wearing a baseball cap. In the two-and-a-half weeks we stayed, her condition had worsened to the point where she couldn't get out of bed. She was obviously a home cancer patient. Big morphine doses.
I went in the studio. She let me add violin to *I Know You by Heart* and that came out beautifully. I played it for her that same evening and she said, 'Well, what you did was good.' She sang impeccably on that tune – that's Eva at her very best. I think she knew she was good, but she was the type of person who was so modest, she would never say so. So she gave me that gift to take away. I was inspired to play beyond my talent and capabilities on that song and that, pretty much in a nutshell, is how Eva affected me musically.

Anna Karen Kristinsdottir It wasn't happy. There were no happy moments. It was just sadness and heaviness and this waiting. There was that slow song that Dan added the violin to and we played it for her. We all went into the room or some of us just stood in the hall and played her that song and she was the only one that wasn't crying. She mentioned that she was very happy with that part – the violin in the song – and she sounded calm. She said, 'Yeah, Dan, this is wonderful.'

Chris Biondo *Eva by Heart* was the album that Eva had been working on that was in the best condition to be finished – that she liked the best. So I took all these things into consideration. Some of the songs on that record were real close or had been finished. Others were really rough rhythm-tracks and some were just a vocal with no music. She had been looking for songs to sing and Al had got a couple of publishers to send him tapes of songs that they had on their catalogues and we found *I Know You by Heart*. She wanted to do *Blues in the Night* and the gospel song, *How Can I Keep From Singing*, we had from before. We'd always wanted to put Dan playing violin in the little instrumental break. These were the songs that were left that were in the best condition to be fixed.

She had really wanted *Waly, Waly* to be done. We didn't really know exactly what she wanted. She had come into the studio a couple of times when Lenny and I were there. She tried playing the strings and I tried playing the strings and Lenny tried playing the strings. I think, I really think, that she'd like it the way it is, but I do not know. But I know that song was the most important to her. That's my favourite. It's real good.

Lenny Williams Eva by Heart was a collection of all these tracks that were just half done or three-quarters done. On *Waly, Waly* we did everything, but even that was based on a conversation that Chris and I had with her about how she envisioned the song to be. *Waly, Waly* was a scratch vocal track she did for me to learn the song and they were always so good. She couldn't sing out of tune. Her pitch was dead on. Her delivery was really well thought out. She knew what she wanted.

Chris Biondo The problem with *Eva by Heart* is Eva's sick and dying and I'm listening to songs about people dying and it's very sad music. A lot of it is really sad on there.

The Cassidys were inundated with friends visiting Eva and calling the house…

Bruce Lundvall I'd got a call saying she was very sick. I was in absolute shock. In the end, I called her. It was the most difficult call I've ever made. Her Mom said, 'Well she's in terrible pain, but I want you to speak to her.' So she put me through and I said, 'I'm really sorry that we never made a record together. It's my fault. Forgive me. I made a terrible mistake,' and she said – she was virtually talking in a whisper, she was in so much pain – 'Look, don't worry, don't even think about it. I don't need to forgive you because we had a wonderful relationship.' And that was it.

Ned Judy Larry called me – told me – 'If you don't come home now, you'll never see her again.' So the next day I got on a plane and came back and by then she was in bed and I never saw her out of bed again. I was in the room with her and the president of Blue Note called, and it was very strange. She was on morphine. She just said, 'Thank you, that's alright,' and she hung up and said, 'That was the president of Blue Note. He was crying, apologising for not having signed me.' She was on morphine. She had less than a week to live at that point.

Bruce Lundvall The whole Eva thing was a painful lesson for me: in the past, I've gone on my instinct and I've usually been proven right. If I heard someone who was original,

'The last day I was there, spontaneously, my Dad, Larry, Ned and I wanted to play once more for Eva.'

Dan Cassidy

I would sign them, and I wouldn't stop to think for a moment how to market them, or what niche to put them into. We should have signed her, and we should have made a record with her.

She was a real artist, one of the great ones. She had the magic – the thing that goes beyond being a really wonderful, creative artist. She had the touch of God on her head – that touch of individuality and spirituality that made her stand out above all the others. She had that. And that's why I was so angry with myself. I would have loved to have made her part of my label's musical legacy, but I completely messed-up, quite frankly.

Herbie Hancock said it best to me. He said: 'You know there are good musicians in every field of music and there are some that are great, really great, but then there are those few

Friends and family play outside Eva's window, October 1996. (from left) Hugh Cassidy, Larry Melton, Dan Cassidy, Ned Judy.

who have that magic, that other dimension, that must come from God,' and that's how I feel about Eva.

Dan Cassidy The last day I was there, spontaneously, my Dad, Larry, Ned and I wanted to play once more for Eva. I was just about to go off to the airport. Eva was bedridden and not conscious very often. We went outside her window, because my mother said, 'Play outside her window – she can hear you.' We lifted ourselves up, played minor swing and old-fashioned, nice, romantic, gypsy-sounding things and apparently, according to what I heard, Eva was singing along, enjoying.

Anna Karen Kristinsdottir I went inside and she was awake and she said she was ready to go in the chair and go outside. It was sunny – it was a beautiful day, but she didn't have the strength and she said, 'I don't want to do it. I don't feel up to it. I'm too tired.' So I said, 'We'll open the window,' and sure enough, that's what we did – they played these songs and it was great. And she laid in the bed and gave instructions and made comments like: 'Dan, do that thing you did!' It was a good thing.

Barbara Cassidy They were all outside at the picnic table and they performed a little concert for her. She was in bed, humming these songs and they were great. She was surrounded by a bubble of love. As long as she could deal with it, she said, 'Oh, let them come,' and they all came.

Chris Biondo Every time we went over there for the last month there'd be people visiting. She'd get really tired because of the company, but people wanted to see her. It was a very sad place – I mean – you'd walk in there and there'd just be people walking around the house crying. It was terrible.

Larry Melton She was so bombarded with visitors. It was so overwhelming, I felt like I'd be doing her a favour by just staying away or just being a sort of presence there, like, 'Hello, hi.' Nothing too heavy. Because she had so many visitors, I can imagine it was exhausting for her. So we didn't really get into much depth at the end. I didn't really know how to handle it so I kind of shut down. I didn't really have the words. I just didn't know what to say. I have regrets about that.

'Her mother asked for Silent Night, and I sang it for her in German. I remember Barbara holding Eva's hand during that, and the look on Eva's face, it was a mixture of wonder and fear. She was wide eyed, like a child, and Barbara was crying.' Grace Griffith

Chris Biondo I think everybody else took it harder than she did. At the point when every bit of news coming down was bad, I can't say how strong she was. She didn't like people being all upset around her. She was sitting in bed, she was still conscious and I was crying. I saw her on the bed and I walked over and she looked up. She said, 'Get over it,' – like, 'You come in here, you can see me, but don't cry and ruin my day. I'm trying to be sick here. I'm trying to get some good sickness done. If you're going to come in and do stupid stuff like that, then don't come in.'

Dan Cassidy There was a lot of commotion, a lot of phone calls. My mother had to screen her calls. It was heart-breaking to see my mother, because she was crying every day. Very tough. My mother was saying, 'Go in and talk to her,' but we didn't have any extended conversations. I did most of the talking. I think I went in two or three times to talk to her. Of course, I'd be getting misty-eyed before I even started talking. She obviously felt bad at all the fuss that was being made and she could see the sadness all around her.

Later that month the family decided to hold an early Christmas celebration for Eva. Grace Griffith, a singer from the Washington DC area, whom Eva held in high esteem, visited…

Barbara Cassidy Oh she got out of bed when Grace came. She had always admired Grace from afar. It was late October and I knew she was going downhill, so I asked them to do some Christmas carols. She did harmonies with those girls and the voice was already weaker, but it was still there. 'My Angel Brigade' she called them.

Grace Griffith I was with my friend Marcy, who is also a singer, and Eva was in a wheelchair. She was wearing a soft beret and looking really beautiful. The family was having an early Christmas and her brother Dan got out his fiddle. Hugh got out his cello, and Eva asked us to sing *My Heart's in the Highlands*, which is a Robert Burns song. Even though Eva was really tired, she came in with this celestial harmony, way up in the top of the range, and it was just such a sweet, sweet thrill to be able to sing with her like that.
Her mother asked for *Silent Night*, and I sang it for her in German. I remember Barbara holding Eva's hand during that, and the look on Eva's face, it was a mixture of wonder and fear. She was wide eyed, like a child, and Barbara was crying. Eva was joining in, but when Barbara started crying she stopped. She was just a little too overcome. I think everyone in the room knew Eva wasn't going to be with us for very long. A lot of times in that situation there is a lot of pretence. When someone is dying, people say: 'Oh, we know you're going to get better,' but this was different.

Kathy Oddenino is a registered nurse and spiritual adviser with many years' experience in counselling the dying…

Kathy Oddenino I give spiritual counselling, and when somebody is as sick as Eva, I go to their home and stay until the pain has gone. I talked to her and let her talk to me. She was a very curious person, who had lots and lots of questions about who she was, about her spirit, about her soul and about the process of dying.

When people are dying, they don't have as many shields up and they open themselves up. They can ask a lot of questions that they need to have answers to. When I first met her, my first impression was how totally spiritual she was without knowing it. She lived a very spiritual type of life. She was not ego-driven, though she did have fear, which we worked on and which she got through before she died.

'Her mother was her saving grace. Her mother was her friend, so consequently when she felt different, she always had her mother that she could turn to.'

Kathy Oddenino

Kathy had the opportunity to discuss in detail Eva's feelings about her life, her thoughts about death and her spiritual beliefs. The Eva she describes is a complex young woman beginning to come to terms with feelings she had struggled with since childhood…

Kathy Oddenino When she was a very small child, she was happy, and she told me the happiest moments of her life were when they were having the family musical sessions and everybody was involved in the music. Playing with the family.

But she had been unhappy for a long, long time. She felt very different, when she was in high school, from kids with their vulgar language and their different kinds of smoking and drinking and all that kind of stuff. They were different from the way she lived her life. So she felt different because she was different.

Her mother was her saving grace. Her mother was her friend, so consequently when she felt different, she always had her mother that she could turn to. When she didn't fit in with this group – didn't fit in with that group – her mother was her stabiliser, her ballast, her best friend and confidante. The way she defined her to me was that she could say anything to her mother and her mother wouldn't judge her or criticise her.

I think the most important thing that she said to me about being different was 'I wanted to be spirit.' She had a belief that as long as you're in your physical body you are not spirit. So, she thought one had to die to become spirit.

Consistent with the recollections of close friends like Anna Karen, Kathy Oddenino describes Eva as a sensitive young woman who found it difficult to express her feelings…

Kathy Oddenino In the early part of her life she never expressed herself. She repressed everything, every feeling, every thought she had. She just thought nobody wanted to hear what she had to say. She did acknowledge to me that there was a lot going through her mind that she wanted to say, and that's very typical of people who have that fear of self-expression – that if they express themselves they're going to be judged. They're going to be inadequate. They're going to be blamed, or unworthy of somebody else's expectations and that's normal. She was very young. It takes people a while to find their own balance in life and she didn't have that kind of time.

There were certain people that she was very, very afraid of creating that kind of situation with, and part of that was her own fear. It doesn't mean the people that she was frightened by intended to frighten her at all. It was her fear that she was dealing with in her own head.

Eva used her music to create a balance and harmony in her life. That was extremely important, and that's why she did only what she wanted to do. She wasn't going to sing to somebody else's dictates if it didn't bring peace and harmony to her.

She looked at it as love. She focused on the words of the song and the love that she felt with the singing. When Eva sang, she sang from her heart, not from her head. Her intention was always to sing her love, to help change other people's lives. She sang because she loved singing and she wanted that song, the sound of her voice, to help change the lives of other people. That's why she never wanted to sing anything except what was coming from her own heart.

Through talking about her feelings with Kathy, Eva was able to find a way to settle any outstanding issues and accept her situation…

Kathy Oddenino During the time that I had been working with her, I helped her see how to face the fear. What she did, and what helped heal her own feelings of worthlessness, was literally to talk to the people that she felt uncomfortable with. By expressing to them the love she really had for them and how she felt, she took away her fear. This works so well; and it always works well with people who are dying, because they know they're up against a time frame. Eva said, 'I wish I had known how to do this, because I could have been doing this and been happier in my life.'

She didn't want to die once she found herself in the position of having melanoma, and knowing that it was throughout her body. At that point she didn't want to die and she didn't want to die for one major reason. She wanted her singing to really impress the people, and then, she knew that if she died, that wasn't going to happen.

I don't think she was afraid of death at all when she died. She told me she wasn't. She knew it was going to happen. She knew she was dying and she was able to talk about it. She wanted to come back living on a farm where she could eat from the land and commune with the trees. She loved nature, so she wanted to be on this farm and she wanted to have a beautiful, wonderful relationship with a man that she could love.

Hugh Cassidy She believed in reincarnation. I think it was comforting – we're going to hook up again. I mean I don't have any doubt about it at all. It may be just a short 'Howdy', because we've all got to get on with our own thing, but reincarnationists believe that the significant people in your life come back again in the form of another entity. I feel we're going to hook up again anyway and, maybe in the interim, we will both have learned something.

Barbara Cassidy She definitely believed in an afterlife and, sort of like Hugh, has the same belief – that life is like a school and if you do a lot wrong you have to come back again to better yourself. One time she said, 'I hope I don't have to come back to do math and science again.'

Ruth Murphy I was pregnant about the time Eva was diagnosed. We found out almost within days of each other. I didn't tell her until I was further along. She was very excited about it. She was really excited about it and that's when she was bringing in the whole reincarnation thing. She was saying: 'I need to call you and Jimmy, Mom and Pop. I would love to come back as your child,' which was sweet stuff. She believed in reincarnation and I think she thought about it sometimes when she sang *Over the Rainbow*. I think it was a core belief for her and I think it influenced a lot of other areas of her life.

Throughout this period Eva's parents, Hugh and Barbara, and her sister, Anette, took responsibility for Eva's day-to-day care...

Anette Cassidy You just do what you have to do to get through it. You don't always think about what you're doing. You just do it. I think we were all in that mode. But I knew it was just breaking Mom's heart, seeing her go downhill so quickly. She was the primary care-giver. Watching your child die is very hard and it was very hard on Dad, too. Mom is better at communicating her feelings and showing her emotions than Dad is. But especially towards the end, I saw a totally different side of him than I had ever seen before. I saw a warm and caring and human side of him. I think it was an event in our family that, of course, was extremely hard; but it's had a lot of good come out of it. We're closer to him.

As the month drew on, the time came for friends and family to say goodbye to Eva...

Anna Karen Kristinsdottir It was late October. I felt that she just gave up, almost as if she knew that it was time. She just couldn't fight it and you could see it – that she was depressed about it, terrified. She wanted me to talk to her and distract her mind – talk about shopping and shoes and colours. I wanted to hold her hand and say things that I really wanted to say. I wanted to say so many things to her and be a huge giver, but I couldn't. I could only talk about stupid things. She liked that though. It made her calm. That's just the way it is.
We didn't really have a conversation, but we hugged and just said, 'Bye.' I can't remember what I said, then I walked

'Mom is better at communicating her feelings and showing her emotions than Dad is. But especially towards the end, I saw a totally different side of him than I had ever seen before. I saw a warm and caring and human side of him. I think it was an event in our family that, of course, was extremely hard; but it's had a lot of good come out of it. We're closer to him.'

Anette Cassidy

slowly out of the room. She didn't talk much. She just lay there, disappearing.

Dan Cassidy Then I had to go in there. It was tough. I knew I'd never see Eva again. But I wasn't shy. I grabbed her hand and said, 'You're going ahead of us. We're going to miss you, but you're going to a good place nonetheless – be brave, be strong.' She said back to me, 'You're really, really good. You're one of the best players I've ever played with. You could play with anyone.' I mean if anyone believed in my music, Eva did, and that goes a long way. I carry that with me wherever I go – Eva's spirit inside of me, especially musically, to excel. That was fantastic. Of course, I was very upset, but I gave her a big hug, very carefully of course. She was very delicate, and that was it.

Larry Melton She was barely in and out of sleep and I just told her I loved her and she said the same thing back. And that seemed a good place to leave it.

Ned Judy I'd been there a week but I had a gig and had to be back in LA. I had to leave on Hallowe'en, October 31st. It was hard. I went in and said, 'I'm leaving now,' and she was out of it because of the morphine. So I started to walk away and the last thing she said was, she came out with, 'Goodbye Ned, have a nice flight,' and that was about all she could say.

Chris Biondo She had gone into a coma but was still responding to stimuli. Like at one point she would grab the little bar that she used to pull herself up on the bed, so Eva was still there a little bit. I just remember the room was real cold and they had this CD of angel music playing and it was just very, very, very, very bad. Everybody was crying.
I was there on the last day, but I did the wrong thing and chickened out at the end. I couldn't stay. I left. I left late afternoon, early evening. Seeing her die, I couldn't do it. I should have been stronger. I should have stayed. There's no doubt about it. I should have actually stayed in that room and waited for her to go. I told Barbara, 'I'm sorry,' and I don't think she even expected me to stay. I think it really would have been the right thing to

stay there, but it was very hard. We expected her to go. We knew she wasn't going to make it through the night.

Barbara Cassidy We had to increase her medication, morphine, and then she had the patch, because you just cannot keep injecting. She slept more and more and more. Then she wanted to hear her records and her music and watched a little bit of television, but she got more and more sleepy and her last words were when her sister Margret checked in on her and she said, 'I love you.'

Margret Cassidy Those were very teary times, which I don't think about too much. I would go in there and sit sometimes and just hold her hand and she'd usually have her eyes closed and I'd be crying. I didn't want her to see me crying because it would get her upset, but I couldn't help it. I was telling her I loved her and she was just like with her eyes closed, 'I love you, too,' in that little voice and I'll never forget that.

Hugh Cassidy Kathy Oddenino came in and volunteered to help her make the passage which she knew by then she was going to pass. Kathy was helping Eva with these little admonitions – these little aphorisms before you go to your sleep – before you go to your rest – thinking positive thoughts – things like that.

Barbara Cassidy The nurse came by that Friday and she said the capacity to take the pain was going and that Eva would pass and it was a good thing. The last two nights Hugh and I just slept in the room, curled on the floor and just slept there. She passed after midnight, the early morning of November 2nd, 1996. We opened a bottle of wine – had a glass of red wine each – toasted her and her new life.

Multimedia picture with dried flowers called 'Looking for Sarah' (Eva's niece).

Dan Cassidy It was just a matter of a waiting game and the night she died I was at a gig ready to play in Iceland and the leader of my band came in. He'd received a call on his mobile from Anna Karen. She'd got the news. He put his hand on my shoulder and said, 'Your sister passed away.' I didn't know what to do and he said, 'Would you like a drink?' I said, 'Yes, a whiskey, please.' I started crying, but I felt good. The next day I talked to my mother and said, 'How do you feel?' and she said, 'Much better. I'm glad it's over.'

Eva was cremated and her ashes taken to St Mary's river…

Barbara Cassidy We scattered her ashes down at St Mary's, one of her favourite spots. In the summer we'd always go swimming there and she'd have a little raft, you know. That was one of her spots. I asked her one time, 'Eva, if you don't survive this, what are we going to do with your body?' and she said, 'I don't want to be in a box. Don't put me in a casket.' And I said, 'How about St Mary's, scattered on the beach?' She said, 'Yes.' She loved that idea. And 'Mom – just make sure I'm really, really dead before I'm cremated.' This was not a frivolous statement, but was made with childlike innocence.

Chris Biondo I remember walking through the woods carrying a little box that had a plastic bag with her ashes in it and walking out on the beach where she used to go rafting. Hugh read a poem and we threw the ashes in the water – took a handful and threw them in the water.

IN THE GOLDEN TIME

The color, the radiance, Child of the sun,
You caused us to see, Daughter of the One,
Would have been missed, May you find your rest
But for your eye In the Golden Time.
That sought tranquility
In the Golden Time. *Hugh Cassidy*
NOVEMBER 17, 1996

On November 19th, 1996, the Cassidys arranged a celebration of Eva's life in Greenbelt Park near their home…

Anette Cassidy My parents wanted to remember the wonderful person that Eva was and celebrate that wonderful person, and celebrate having the opportunity to know her.

Chris Biondo It was November and a little chilly out yet it was packed with people. Probably about half a dozen people said things. It was just a really, really nice thing and very well attended by all colours, creeds and denominations. She was colour-blind and there were so many people from all of the different styles of music. She was appreciated for exactly what she was, which was a beautiful person.

For Eva's friends and family, the process began of coming to terms with the loss…

Margret Cassidy There's an expression that I hear sometimes that I told my mother reminds me of Eva – when they say someone's a very old soul. I think just in her short time

---

A Service of Memory and Celebration for Eva Cassidy

1 p.m. Tuesday, November 19.1996

Ingathering Music

Opening Words Linda Olson Peebles, Minister

"Scottish Laments" Dan Cassidy, Violinist

Prayer and Meditation

Sharings John Cassidy, Ruth Murphy
& Jim Dickey, Larry Hurley,
Mark Merella

"Hearth and Fire" Celia Murphy

Sharings Barry Robinson, Al Dale,
Charles Cassel, Monica Steiner

"Golden Threads" Grace Griffith

Reflections & Benediction Linda Olson Peebles

Toast "Do Lord!" by Eva Cassidy

****

Fellowship Music by Eva Cassidy

on earth, she had acquired so much knowledge and perspective, that her time on earth was done. I think it was just so good in the end that she got all that recognition, that she could leave remembering that. And I think she had forgiven everybody for everything a long time before and her only regret was leaving, because Mom would be sad.

Eva was always following her own path and I can picture her just by herself walking along a path – enjoying flowers and butterflies along the way, and whatever animals would be there. So now that I think about it, it was just like a journey: Eva came here and she did what she did, and then it was time to go.

Anette Cassidy Her friends were all so supportive. She had some wonderful, wonderful friends and they were just there for her all the time. I think that says a lot about the kind of person Eva was – having such good friends. I think she really was a special person. And I was quite angry for a long time that she was taken away from me before I got to know her.

Larry Melton There are things that remind me – there are little jokes and sayings that we had together that only she and I know – that remind me of her. The thing I miss the most is her sense of humour and how easily she would laugh at my stupid jokes and my imitations, because I'd do a lot of voice characters and we'd just make up characters. That's the thing I miss the most – that sort of connection. I was really crazy about her and I thought the best way to really connect was to keep her laughing: 'She'll really, really like me if I just keep her laughing.' So that was my deal. So those are the things I miss the most.

Anna Karen Kristinsdottir She loved animals. She felt if she could have been an animal herself, she would have – free as a bird. She loved birds. If she could have been an animal or a bird, then she would have been able to fly off – just take off, do her stuff – be herself and be free. *Over the Rainbow* – somewhere where it's peaceful and beautiful.

Ruth Murphy I was four months pregnant when I spoke at her funeral, so it was very short from the time I got pregnant to her passing away. Our daughter Cassidy is named after Eva. She is very much an artist, loves to paint, loves to draw. She's very temperamental, so she shares that in common with Eva, and she always loved Eva's music as a baby, particularly *Wade in the Water*. Just the other day, in the morning when I was cooking breakfast, Cassidy said, 'Mom, put on the Eva CD.' Cassidy will grow up with Eva.

Hugh Cassidy We were in a pretty good place when she passed and if she had continued living, I think we would have been a bunch of comfortable, connected folks, really doing a lot of stuff together. I could see that happening, because you never stop growing. You get together now or you get together later, but eventually you get together if you both have your sights set on it. Of course, I had no doubts that she was interested in being my daughter and I her father. We were working on it, but we lost that potential. One of the joys of living is to watch your children grow up and become – what we lost was the chance to see her grow and see her become something more than she already was.

I have a little tape from when she was ill and I still have this little tape where she was speaking to herself once in this little recorder. She said, 'When I get well, I'm gonna go out into the woods, I'm gonna hike and I'm gonna bike and I'm gonna have fun in the sunshine.' So I guess that's what she'd be doing now.

I knew Eva always had a thing for angels and cherubs and little babies and innocence and purity. She bought little angel figurines and collected them. She visited cemeteries and churches and places that had them. When she was on her deathbed, I mentioned that I was going to make an angel for her. She said, 'That's nice,' but I didn't complete it until a month after her passing. I had begun making a woman's face out of clay and then poured aluminium in there. After I had sanded the casting down, I was amazed to see how closely it resembled Eva. We look at that face every time we look out of the window, and we see her face shining.

I had wonderful visions of, perhaps, maybe as a trio we would get together: Dan, Eva and myself. It would have been nice. It would have been beautiful – cello, violin and guitar and her singing and she would've been the boss. She'd have been in charge and calling what she wanted and we would have been only happy to make her shine. I had visions of that and I regret very much that it did not come to be.

Barbara Cassidy When I hear *I Know You by Heart*, this is Eva and me; and *Fields of Gold* is Eva and me out there in the meadow picking flowers. It just describes it all perfectly. I got so much from the relationship. I feel I was blessed.

'I knew Eva always had a thing for angels and cherubs and little babies and innocence and purity. She bought little angel figurines and collected them. She visited cemeteries and churches and places that had them. When she was on her deathbed, I mentioned that I was going to make an angel for her. She said "that's nice", but I didn't complete it until a month after her passing.' Hugh Cassidy

Songbird

It goes without saying that the last thing Hugh and Barbara Cassidy were thinking about as their daughter lay dying, was whether or not she was going to make it in the record business. But ironically the key moment of Eva's professional career happened during those last, painful days. The moment that triggered her journey from relative obscurity to best-selling stardom was a phone call, made by Grace Griffith to Bill Straw. Bill was Grace's friend, and the boss of her record label: a small, independent outfit called Blix Street Records, based in Hollywood…

Grace Griffith I was talking to Bill about some record company stuff and I broke off from what I was saying and said something like, 'Look, before I go on, I just want to tell you, we have this wonderful angel, this wonderful nightingale, that I'm afraid we're going to lose.' I asked him if I could send him a tape of Eva singing, and he said, 'Sure.'

Bill Straw Grace is not someone who says things lightly. When she says something, you listen. So the tape arrives, and it's the *Live at Blues Alley* album, cued up to *Fields of Gold*. So I put it on and of course I was blown away. It took just five seconds. I sat there and listened to the whole thing and I just knew it, there wasn't a pop singer out there who could touch her. But I also knew that she was dying, so the last thing on my mind was business. I just thought, 'Oh my God, this girl is going to be famous and she isn't going to be around to enjoy it.' I wanted to meet her, but it just didn't seem like the right thing to do, to ask to see someone who was dying. In retrospect, I wish I had. I asked Grace what

Eva's parents wanted to do with the music – because I felt it was important that the world hear the music – because there was such a healing aspect to it.

Bill Straw played the tape to his old friend, Martin Jennings, the Managing Director of Hot Records, an independent UK record label…

Martin Jennings I'd known Bill Straw from the 1970s, when we used to work together at Warner Records. I'd often pop over and see him on my travels. In spring 1997 I was at Bill's house in Los Angeles, hanging out, when Bill popped a tape on, without saying anything. He does this quite often, like he's testing me. A lot of the time I'll say nothing, but this time, after only a few seconds, I said, 'Bill, who's that?' and then he tells me the whole story. It did my head in: on the one hand I couldn't get over the sound of this fantastic singer, but then at the same time there was this terribly sad tale. I've been in the record business all my life and, believe me, you don't hear voices like Eva's every day. It was amazing really – her voice just stuck out, like a beacon. It was the quality that did it, the pureness and her phrasing. As Miles Davis says, 'It's not where the notes are; it's where the notes aren't.' And Eva leaves gaps in the most unusual places, like on her version of *Over the Rainbow*. That's how she managed to make it sound so different from the Judy Garland version. Anyway, I just went, 'Wow,' It really floored me, actually. So I asked all the questions, like you do – like: 'Has she got any records out? Where can I get them?' and Bill told me he was going to see Eva's parents to talk about the rights to her songs. So I wished Bill the best of luck and gave him plenty of encouragement over the next few months.

Bill Straw After a few months Grace arranged for me to meet the Cassidys, and we all went out to dinner. I didn't come over all strong with them, saying, 'Let's do the deal right here,' and that kind of thing, because it just didn't seem right. But they wanted her music to be released and so eventually we got a deal done. One day I went to Chris Biondo's studio, and I heard the rest of her stuff, and that's when I got the idea for the *Songbird* album. I didn't want to do a *Best of Eva Cassidy* record. I wanted something that would sound coherent, a good mix. I knew we had to start it with *Fields of Gold* and end it with *Over the Rainbow*. The only other question then was, what should we put in between. What makes a record good is not necessarily what you put in, but what you leave out, and we left some great things off *Songbird*, like *Wonderful World*. I just didn't think it fit with the other tracks.

Martin Jennings So there we are, in the spring of 1998, and *Songbird* is finally out, and I'm responsible for breaking it in Europe and Australasia. The first thing I realise is, 'This has got to be plugged properly.' I mean, you can't expect to walk into any old radio station with a record like that and just say, 'Play this,' and expect them to play it, because it just doesn't work like that. I knew right away that Radio 2 might be a good bet, so I sent Andrew Bowles, who worked for me, to go and see them. But he didn't get very far. To be honest, I don't think the guys at Radio 2 respond very well to having a young bloke telling them what's good or not. They need someone of their own age to sell it to them. Anyway, I racked my brains for months trying to think of someone and I came up with

Tony Bramwell, a guy I'd known since 1973. For years he was the top record plugger in the world, really. But could I find him? No way.

I'd seen him around in bars in the 1980s, where we'd have the odd beer, but no one seemed to know where he'd got to. Eventually I tracked him down to Devon.

Tony Bramwell I'd virtually stopped plugging altogether by this time. There was nothing I was really interested in any more. I'd been there, done that, I suppose. I'd worked for some of the biggest names in the business – the Beatles, Roxy Music, Phil Spector, the Jam, Slade – and to be honest, I'd grown a bit tired of it all. I wasn't really into the way the big record companies had let the marketing take over from the music. It just wasn't my bag of bananas any more. After thirty years I'd just got fed up with being nice to people. I had got involved in other things – like starting my own record label.

Martin Jennings I didn't tell him Eva's story or anything. I just said, 'Would you mind having a listen.'

Tony Bramwell I wasn't exactly straining at the leash, I must admit. I felt a bit like one of those retired gunslingers that John Wayne used to play, who'd been persuaded to make one last comeback. The first tracks I heard were *Fields of Gold* and *Wonderful World* and they got me, completely. It was like – 'I know these songs, but they don't sound like the way I know them.' I've always been a great song man and a lot of the ones that Eva had covered were in my all-time favourites. I thought, not only is there a brilliant voice here, but there's a brilliant arranger, too.

She'd actually totally deconstructed the songs. The problem, of course, was that it didn't fit into any genre. It wasn't the Corrs, it wasn't Madonna, and anyway, there wasn't any money to market her like those acts. But the quality just shone through.

I left the tape alone for a few hours then went back to it – just to check that my instincts were right. And when I heard it again, I thought, 'Well, if this was the sixties, this artist would be right up there with James Taylor, Carole King and the like.'

Martin Jennings Tony rang me the night he received the package and said, 'This should be all over Radio 2.' So we arranged to meet in London.

Tony Bramwell We met at a pub at lunchtime and talked about old times and got slightly pissed, actually. He brought me a box full of copies of *Songbird* and at around 5pm, I wandered into Radio Two and started doling them all out. Then I got the train back to Devon. I have to say I was quite excited, actually, as it was the first time I'd done a bit of plugging for ten years. The next day I sent a small note to some of the people I knew from the old days, who I knew would trust my judgment – like Paul Walters, Terry Wogan's producer, and said, 'Sorry to bother you, but I think this is actually rather great.'

Paul Walters I get a pile of records to listen to every day – I mean there's normally two or three hundred stacked up on my desk, waiting to be heard. But I knew Tony. He's not

one to say something is good when it isn't. In my job you really value that. He wouldn't give you crap. He's been around a long time and he's got the right idea. So I stuck it on, and played the track he recommended, *Over the Rainbow*. And it absolutely stopped me in my tracks.

Tony Bramwell Two days later I got a fax from Paul Walters saying something like, 'Bloody brilliant! It was no bother listening to something like this. The choice of songs is fantastic. We're going with it tomorrow.'

Paul Walters It was one of those very rare moments – I mean I've been in the business since 1963 – where you think, 'Oh Jeez,' and put it back to the top in order to listen to it properly, rather than just sitting there and listening to it while you answer emails or something. I was absolutely stunned. I listened to the whole album. I was just totally gobsmacked. I thought she was sensational. It was one of those voices which, to me, was as distinctive and pure as say, Karen Carpenter. Or Streisand. The kind of voice which, with the right song, can just make you sit up and listen. And that's the beauty of radio, as opposed to telly: if you like something you can start pushing it immediately, like, overnight. So that's what I did, basically: I went in to work the next morning and said to Terry, 'You wait till you hear this, matey.'

'The kind of voice which, with the right song, can just make you sit up and listen.'

Paul Walters

Terry Wogan Paul's got good ears, as he'll tell you himself. But I have to say I really didn't know what to expect.

Paul Walters I must admit, at this stage, when we were about to play the record for the first time, I didn't know she was dead. I hadn't read the sleeve notes or anything. I remember Terry introducing it, saying something like, 'OK, this is one Paulie's brought in this morning by a lady called Eva Cassidy. Hope you like it.' And he put it on. And it had the same effect on him as it had on me.

Terry Wogan Hundreds of records get brought to my attention every month, but this stood out immediately. Extraordinary voice. Perfect pitch. Extraordinary in that it had a quality you don't hear very often – once in a blue moon. It would have been obvious to anybody, I'd have thought. It was certainly obvious to Paul and me. We just sat there, listening to it. It was only when I was browsing through the sleeve notes that I realised the whole story and said something like, 'Hey Paul, you do know she's dead, don't you?'

Paul Walters I was gobsmacked. I had no idea. Terry handled it very well though, at the end of the song he went on about how brilliant it was and said something like, 'That was Eva Cassidy, who it seems is tragically no longer with us.' Well, I mean the e mails lit up like a Christmas tree. Sometimes I'll get two or three asking about a song, but after this we got more than one hundred in ten minutes, which is just unprecedented.
Then I get back to the office after the show and the lights are flashing on my phone and my secretary's, and there are faxes as well, all wanting to know what it was. Then of course the post comes in. I mean, we ended up having to make a standard reply to cope with it all. You know – 'Thank you for your enquiry. The song was *Over the Rainbow* by Eva Cassidy, CD number blah, blah' – that sort of thing. The great thing is, because of who Terry is, I have a pretty free hand when it comes to music. So I thought, well, I'm going to play this whenever I like. Because other people in the building, although they liked it, it didn't really have enough street cred for them. Do you know what I mean? It was a bit too conservative for them. So it was really a bit of a lone crusade at the start. But then, after a couple of weeks of us playing two or three tracks, other people started playing it – like Michael Parkinson and Bob Harris, and even Steve Wright, I think.

Martin Jennings So there we are, just three of us, running the company out of a little cottage in Angmering in Sussex; and suddenly it's starting to happen. From nothing, we're suddenly getting orders for, like, two thousand copies of *Songbird* a week. It was really exciting. But it was frustrating. too. We got to Number 78 in the charts just before Christmas 1998. To get attention from the press though, you need to get in the top 75. After Christmas the record started dropping back down again, but it never went away. Radio 2 kept playing it, and the word of mouth was amazing. I knew we were on to something, because of the feedback we were getting from punters. They were sending us emails all the time. I remember one that said, 'I've never been struck by someone's voice so much since I first heard Billie Holiday,' That really kept us going. And the record shops were telling us good things, too. That's the good thing about being independent: because we distribute our own records we have our ears really close to the ground and can pick up on what's going on out there much quicker than the big boys.

Songbird kept on selling: by late 2000 it had gone Gold, having shifted more than 100,000 copies. There was delight, but also frustration. Because those sales were steady, not spectacular, it still hadn't got into the top 75. If only they could get past that magic number, the album would inevitably get far more attention from the press and reach an even wider audience. Tony Bramwell decided that the key was to try and get the video of Eva singing *Over the Rainbow* onto mainstream television…

Tony Bramwell When I first saw the film of Eva playing *Over the Rainbow* I thought, 'Well, that's nice. It'll make a nice piece of documentary footage, but it's going to be hard to get it on a music show.' I went round showing it to people, but no one went for it. But then I bumped into a guy called Mark Hagen, who I vaguely knew, sitting in the lobby at the BBC. At the time he was producing Top of the Pops 2. So I asked him if he'd have a look at it, and he said, 'Sure.'

Mark Hagen I'd known Tony for years. And I was aware of Eva, from Terry's show. And he gives me this footage and it's, like, dreadful – I mean terrible, by any conventional standards. Not the music – I mean the quality of the film: grainy, black-and-white, shot on a single camera – that kind of thing. And it was five-and-half minutes long! So I gave it a cursory look to start with and said, 'Well, I'm sorry Tony. People aren't going to watch this.'

Tony Bramwell Occasionally I'd see Mark and say, 'Come on, isn't it time you played it' and he always used to – kind of snigger a bit. But I kept on grinding him down and around about November 2000, I reminded him that it was the anniversary of Eva's death. He said, 'Oh really?' and I said, 'Yeah,' and he said, 'OK, I give up. I'll show it.'

Mark Hagen He kept on at me. He's very tenacious like that. I realised it was worth taking a chance on, as it was such a fantastic performance. I knew I would risk losing some of the audience, but I thought it was a risk worth taking, as it might keep more people than it lost. Anyway I played it before Christmas. I put it at the end of the show, as that's where I put stuff that's new. Also, if everyone else says, 'Oh my God, this is dreadful,' and switches off, it doesn't destroy your ratings.

Tony Bramwell I told him he could get away with it, but I think he was worried what the reaction would be if they showed what was basically a home video of a dead girl singing a song that wasn't a hit. Of course, there were lots of other videos around from the big record companies – videos that cost a fortune. But when he finally played it, the reaction was incredible.

Mark Hagen Well, really, I've never had a response like it! I mean the day after, I took probably two hundred calls, and there were loads more calls to the BBC duty office, and emails, things like that. The next day, I got a load more, and the next day – and this actually went on until January. People would ring me and say, 'You know that blonde girl you had on a couple of months ago…' and I'd butt in and say, 'Eva Cassidy, *Over the Rainbow*,' and they'd say, 'Thanks very much,' and ring off. In the end we had thousands and thousands of enquiries. There were so many I never got round to counting them all. I was flabbergasted… I really didn't expect it! We'd had nothing like this, ever. There was one letter I got, from a retired Army-type, who said that he'd just heard Eva on the radio and he'd cried. He said it was the first time in his life that a piece of music had made him cry. Incredible.

Martin Jennings Until Mark played it on TV we couldn't get the press remotely interested. Then he puts it on, just before Christmas 2000, and everyone goes bonkers. Overnight, we start getting calls from ITN, the BBC, the national papers, Richard and Judy, GMTV – everyone wanted to do the story. Even *Time* magazine. The funny thing was, the video was just a grainy black-and-white thing – the complete antithesis of all those million-dollar things you see on MTV. I think it was the low-tech-ness of it all that captured people's imaginations – apart from her incredible performance, of course. It was so far behind, it was in front. It was like, 'Wow, what a great idea. Let's get a girl, and a guitar, and sit her down on a stool, and get her to sing.' It was a kind of back-to-basics thing, really. If we'd done the big record company thing and spent loads of money tarting it up, we'd have ruined it.

Tony Bramwell The thing about the video was, it was so blatantly different. And, of course, the song means a lot of things to a lot of people. I think a lot of them had heard the song on Wogan, or on local radio, and they were then able to make that connection – to put the face to the voice – and that was quite a powerful thing.

Mark Hagen I think there was a vague awareness of Eva, because of Terry playing the record all the time. But I think what really made it take off was that people got this chance to see her. That was when they got the whole picture. The key, I think, was that you could see she wasn't just singing the song – she was thinking it, she was feeling it. That's why she's such an amazing talent. There's no gap between the emotion and the performance. There's no sense that it's being filtered through some kind of artistic sensibility and then reproduced. It goes straight from her to whoever is listening. There's no intermediary. And, of course, it was a song that everyone knew. That helped. They had something to compare it against.

Martin Jennings Anyway they played the video and the publicity started exploding. The *Songbird* CD shot into the charts in the New Year, at Number 33. Then it went to 19 the next week. Then 18, then 3. I remember being in Australia that week and getting a call from Tony at 2.30 in the morning and all he could say was, 'We're at Number Three! We're at Number Three!' Then *Tonight With Trevor McDonald* went and did this fantastic report about the whole Eva story and, hey presto! Three days later, we're Number One. I was beside myself.

Tony Bramwell It was my birthday the week before it got to Number One. My kids had been on their computers a lot, charting the record's progress on Amazon, saying, 'Hey Dad, it's Number Three, hey Dad, it's Number Two.' But when it finally hit the top of the official charts it was just, like, 'Wow.' It was really quite incredible. So me and the Missus went and opened a bottle of champagne to celebrate. I felt very proud. It's always great to have success with a total outsider – to have your hunch proved right. I mean, I'd spent so long telling everyone about her, trying to get them interested and then – all of a sudden people were calling from all over the world saying, 'You were right, you scouse git.' I have to say, an air of smugness was apparent. Of all the acts I've ever handled, this one has given me the most pleasure, because it was such a long shot. She had no chance, but she made it.

Sting I'd been sent a cassette and a letter explaining that this girl, Eva Cassidy, had died, and would I listen to her rendition of *Fields of Gold*. I get a lot of tapes, you know, but I was so moved by the letter, that I thought, OK, I'll listen to it. Normally I'll give it eight bars and if it hasn't moved me by then, I'll go on to the next one. So I heard this voice, and it was so beautiful, so pure. And then I reread the letter, and I played the song to my wife, and she said, 'It's fantastic.' But I said, 'I don't think there's anything we can do with it, but it's nice to have been privy to that performance.' And the next thing I hear, it's almost a year later, and Terry Wogan is playing *Fields of Gold* on Radio 2, and I think; 'Great, that's really nice. Somebody else has thought this is beautiful, too.' And then, lo and behold – it's the Number One album in England. And I'm very happy for her. Even though it's a sad tragic story, it has a kind of poetry about it.

Bill Straw I always thought she would do better in Britain than in America, because of your national radio system. In the States she has been selling well, but it's like, mini-explosions here and there. The trouble is: in America getting on the radio isn't about music; it's about money.

Within weeks of the video being played on television, *Songbird* had sold more than 900,000 copies, and gone Platinum. In the first three months of 2001 in the UK, Eva outsold every single artist in the world, apart from Dido. Her other albums have sold well, too, with *Time After Time* now having passed the 150,000 mark.

And her popularity isn't confined to Britain. She is selling heavily in Australia, Germany, and particularly – for reasons the staff at Hot Records cannot quite fathom, but are nevertheless delighted about – Switzerland. And there are signs that America is finally beginning to 'get' Eva, too. There have been stories about her in the national press and on the mainstream current affairs show, *Nightline…*

Mark Hagen There was this amazing word-of-mouth thing that happened with Eva. People bought the record, then told all their friends about it. And people kept buying it because they weren't being saturated with it on the radio. There wasn't the overkill you get with some records. And also, with a lot of radio-friendly music these days, you don't need to buy it, as everything you want from it you can get just by listening to it on the

'So I heard
this voice, and
it was so
beautiful,
so pure.'

Sting

radio. It's not going to stand up to you playing it for four or five years at home. Whereas this, you can play it over and over again and it will work on different levels.

Martin Jennings The effect on my business was amazing. Before Eva, we were just getting by. One moment we were in a cottage – the next there was about twenty of us in a big barn down the road. We couldn't stay in the cottage as it was causing problems. When the blokes from TNT used to deliver Eva's CDs, they would leave them in huge cartons, piled high in the road, just outside the front gate. But the road wasn't very wide, so once or twice it actually caused a mini traffic jam.

Paul Walters Had she not been dead, I still think she would have been an enormous success. Because they're good songs and people would still have bought them. I would have gone through exactly the same process I went through, and played her stuff, regardless. Of course, that publicity helped hugely, I mean as far as the press was concerned, her not being around any more was the story. Had she lived, she would still have made it, but perhaps not in quite as big a way as she has.

Martin Jennings She might well have made it. It's not impossible. I mean Raymond Chandler didn't write his first novel till he was in his forties, and Al Jarreau didn't make a record until he was thirty-six. No one will ever know. But it's not like we went to Radio 2 and said, 'Here's this terribly sad story. Play this record.' It was: 'Here's a great record. See what you think.' They played it because it was really good. It's as simple as that.

Tony Bramwell The British record-buying public is phenomenal. They are subjected to all this stuff that's rammed down their throats and hyped up in the tabloids all the time, but they still have this ability to take something that is completely outside all that and make it their own – which is what they did with Eva.

Martin Jennings I'm really pleased that we, the British public, discovered Eva before anyone else. I remember when artists like Chuck Berry couldn't take off in America – he used to play behind chicken wire, in fact – but then he took off over here and suddenly people in the USA and all over the world caught on. The same thing's happened with Eva and I'm really proud of it. It proves British people have ears, and taste. I don't think Eva's going to go away, either – she's too good! She had this incredible ability to take on a really well-known song and make it sound like her own.

Mick Fleetwood The British people and the British press really deserve a round of applause for allowing someone who so went against the grain to make it. It was all down to her voice, and some people having the balls to play it on the radio.

'People wrote to me who had lost loved ones

or had love affairs go sour, and this music buoyed

them through some tough times.'

Hugh Cassidy

Time is a Healer

Five years after her death Eva Cassidy became a star. But how will
history treat her? Is she just this year's thing, or will people still be
listening to her music in fifty years? The early signs are encouraging.
A poll of listeners, songwriters and music-industry experts
commissioned by BBC Radio 2 in the spring of 2001, rated Eva number
twenty-one in the list of the one hundred best voices of all time.
She was in good company: just behind Ella Fitzgerald, Aretha Franklin
and Billie Holiday, and ahead of Judy Garland, Karen Carpenter,
Sarah Vaughan and her hero, Stevie Wonder.

In the Radio 2 poll of the one hundred most memorable songs of all
time, *Over the Rainbow* came in at Number Nine, but as many people
voted for Eva's version as Judy Garland's. And it was Eva's version of the
song that was chosen by the makers of *Coronation Street* in June 2001
as the music for Alma's funeral…

Terry Wogan Such is the quality of her voice, she makes everything
stand out. Occasionally, when we play her version of *Over the
Rainbow*, we get listeners writing in to say, 'Play the Judy Garland
version,' and yes, of course Judy's version is probably one of the
outstanding records of all time. But Eva's version is different –
distinctive – and beautiful.

Paul Walters Her great achievement, I think, is *Over the Rainbow*. I mean, she's done the impossible and redefined a standard. To people of a certain age, that song is Judy Garland's, and quite rightly. But then suddenly, along comes someone else; and for a big percentage of people, Eva Cassidy's version is now the definitive version. I mean, I grew up with Judy Garland being around, and I could appreciate what a good song it was; but it was always a bit showbizzy for me. But then along comes Eva and all of a sudden that song is real for me. And the reason is the simplicity. It wasn't five trumpets, five trombones, a rhythm section and a big arrangement. It was just a girl and a guitar. And she didn't just sing it, she thought it, too. You get the feeling that the song could still make her cry, even though she'd sung it hundreds and hundreds of times – because she loved it so much.

Terry Wogan One of the reasons why *Over the Rainbow* touches so many people is, of course, because of the film *The Wizard of Oz*. It's a film that everyone has seen – everyone of a certain age, that is. Then, of course, Judy Garland had such a romantic image, and a tragic life. Of course, Eva's tragedy can't be discounted – this brilliant singer, unrecognised while she was alive, but now a star after her death. All these things – the history of the song and its singers – give it a quality that attracts people. You would have thought, after the Garland version, 'Nobody could possibly sing this song,' and yet Eva gives it something extra, something different. She gives it herself. It's almost sinful to say so, because Judy Garland is such an icon; but I prefer Eva's version.

Mark Hagen My mother is very ill at the moment. She's dying, and *Over the Rainbow* has a completely different resonance for me, compared to what it felt like before. Eva's music is very simple. But that's its strength. It's so simple, it's complicated.

Mick Fleetwood I love her version of *Over the Rainbow*. It's the sweetest thing you ever heard. I often listen to her music, me and my wife. It brings back a lot of memories.

Martin Jennings It's funny. I should be used to Eva by now, but I'm not. I believe she's a once-in-a-lifetime artist. I still get goose bumps, even now, when I hear *Over the Rainbow*, after all these years. In fact, I always will. She's going to be around forever, I think. She's going to be one of the all-time greats.

Tony Bramwell She isn't going to be a flash in the pan. Because she's brilliant! She's a fixture in people's lives now, in much the same way that Princess Di was, I suppose. There's such an emotional depth in her songs – people really make a connection with her. You only have to look at some of the outpourings on her websites to see that. She's struck a chord. She's going to be a legend.

Sting A lot of people have covered my songs. And it's a strange emotion, you know, because your own songs are like your own babies. I mean you might hear someone reinterpreting them and maybe you don't agree with what they've done. But this version was just so pure, so excellent, that I was deeply moved by it, and so happy that she'd covered it. Eva's is one of the best versions of my song I've ever heard.

Terry Wogan Her voice is perfect! When you hear other people on record, they've spent weeks or months, in the studio. It's been overdubbed, it's been re-recorded, overdubbed again, polished and honed to fine perfection. Just about everything you hear Eva Cassidy do, has been done live. That's what makes it outstanding.

Mick Fleetwood I rate her incredibly highly. It's very, very hard to interpret other people's songs and still make it sound like your own. Eva had that. Frank Sinatra had that quality – the song almost became his property because it was so uniquely his. She had that ability, too, which I believe to be very rare. I believe she will go on to become one of the all-time greats. Even though she hasn't left a very large body of work behind, I get a lot of feedback from people who just say how moved they are by her singing. That's the description I always get from people about Eva. They are moved by her, and that goes a long long way in terms of creating a legacy, which I hope and believe she will.

Bill Straw We have a lot more material that we could release, but we have to be careful. I don't want to be accused of scraping the barrel. I want to add to her legend, not tarnish it. I think there will be another album – we are talking about doing one called *Legendary Pearls*, which has some stuff on it that no one has heard – like a great version of a Gordon Lightfoot song called *Early Morning Rain*. We have a version of *Imagine*, and *Yesterday*, too. But I'm going to be patient. I want to get the right album out. I don't want to just throw something together.

Sting There is something about her voice – a quality – that you can't really put into words. It's a magical quality. People respond to its purity. It suggests something ethereal – something unattainable.

Meanwhile, back in Bowie, the Cassidys found themselves having to deal with

the consequences of their daughter's amazing success. Hugh and Barbara now found themselves inundated with media enquiries and letters from fans…

Hugh Cassidy The response was overwhelmingly wonderful and did a lot to remove the sting of her death. It's good closure for us when we read these letters. We get a lot of comfort from them. People wrote to me who had lost loved ones or had love affairs go sour, and this music buoyed them through some tough times.
A waitress in Ireland said she enjoys watching the pub quiet down on a Saturday night, when there are usually a raucous bunch of guys in. Suddenly they stop what they are doing when they hear Eva's voice on *Over the Rainbow*. She says it's a calming thing. She gets a kick out of seeing their faces change – and watching their demeanour change from these normally loud and aggressive people – as it works its magic on them.

Barbara Cassidy It's very gratifying, the effect she has had on people, and the wonderful letters we have received. When people sit down and write a heartfelt letter, that is wonderful. It's still hard to believe sometimes – there's Eva my child and now Eva the famous singer and I just haven't put the two together yet. It's going to take a while for me.

Anette Cassidy I am very proud. It's the kind of thing you never think will happen in your family. But there is still anger and sadness that she was taken away from us so young – just when things were finally on the right track. I just can't make any sense of it.

Dan Cassidy I don't think she would have cracked under the pressure, but you never know. She may have looked for excuses not to let it get as big as this. It wasn't important to her, fame. She never talked about, 'Some day I'm going to be big'. She was the antithesis of Madonna.

Anette Cassidy She wouldn't have enjoyed the fuss at all. One of the options, of course, would have been to walk away from it all and that wouldn't have surprised me at all. Success, fame and fortune weren't on the top of her list of priorities.

Chris Biondo Looking down on us right now and seeing what's going on, I think she'd be totally amazed. I don't think she, in her wildest dreams, would think that her record would come out, go to England, go to Number One, and they'd be making television shows about her. I don't think it was really in her nature to have an appetite for stardom – to be a person that is paid a lot of attention.

Barbara Cassidy You know, I don't listen to her music much now on a regular basis. I have to be just in the right mood. Hugh plays her much more often and when he does, he plays his cello along with her music. But when we want to remember Eva we sometimes go to a stretch of water, a lake, about an hour's drive from the house, where Eva and I used to come to bicycle. I can almost feel her presence, the beauty of it, and it gives me a very special, peaceful yet emotional feeling. She was a very, very special person, I guess – but not just to me, and now the whole world is beginning to realise that.

The Song of Life

Come join the dance of Life!
    Hear the magic drum and fife.
      Lift your feet
        To the lively beat . . .
          and dance!

Lift your voice in song,
    And I will sing along.
      Come, take my hand!
        We're in the big band
          of Life.

The beat is now and fast.
    How long will our song last?
      Who cares, as long as we
      Can sing in harmony
        right now!

Let's teach this song to others —
    Sisters, daughters, mothers —
      Fathers, sons and brothers!
        When one voice ends,
        Another blends
          in song.

Let's dance until we drop!
    Don't let the music stop . . .
      One voice is gone.
        But not the song
          of Life.

Elana Rhodes Byrd